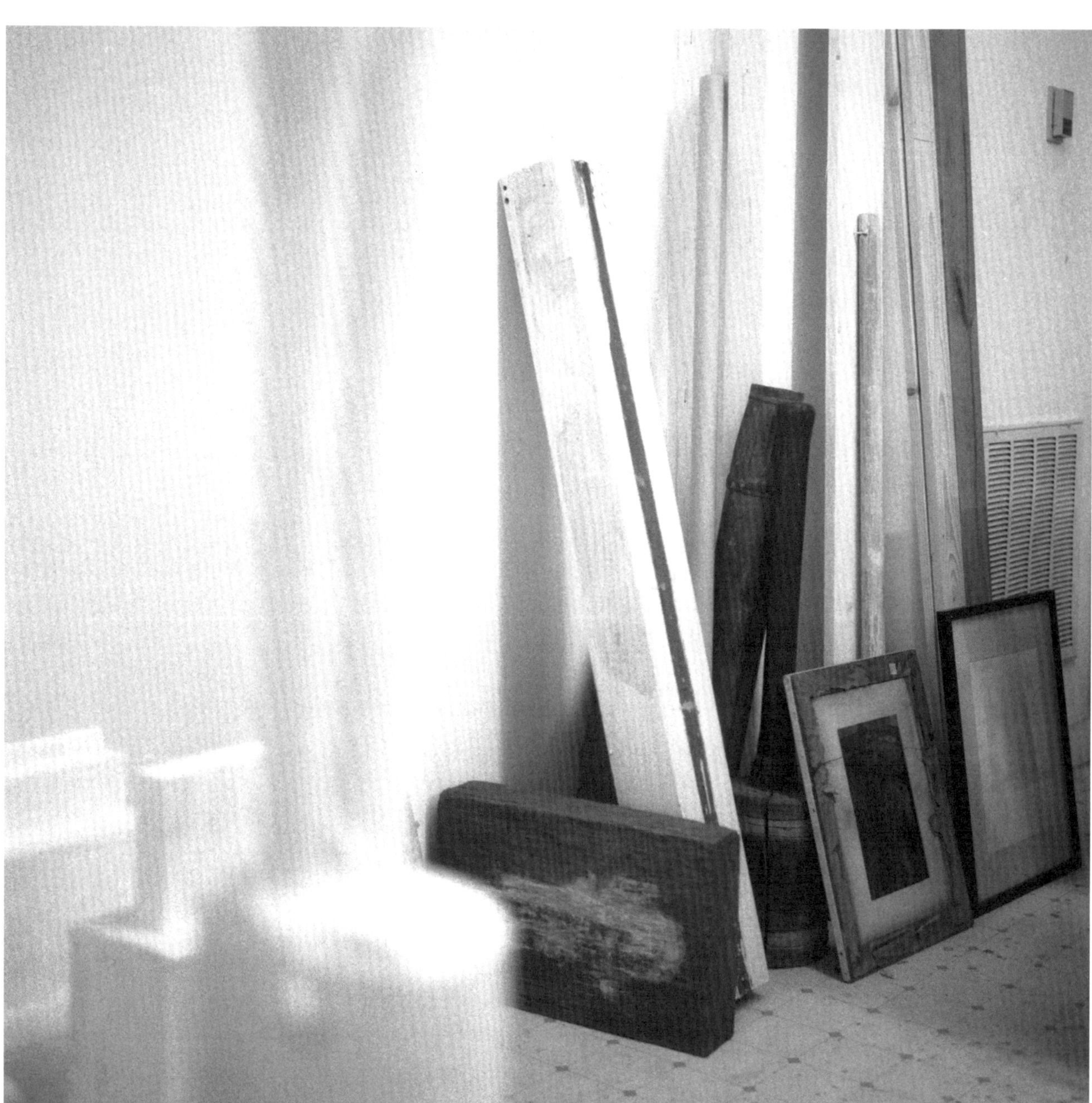

STUDIO NOTES – MY TIME WITH CY

Photographs by Rob McDonald

Text by Sam Stephenson
Essay by Thierry Greub

Verlag der Buchhandlung Walther und Franz König

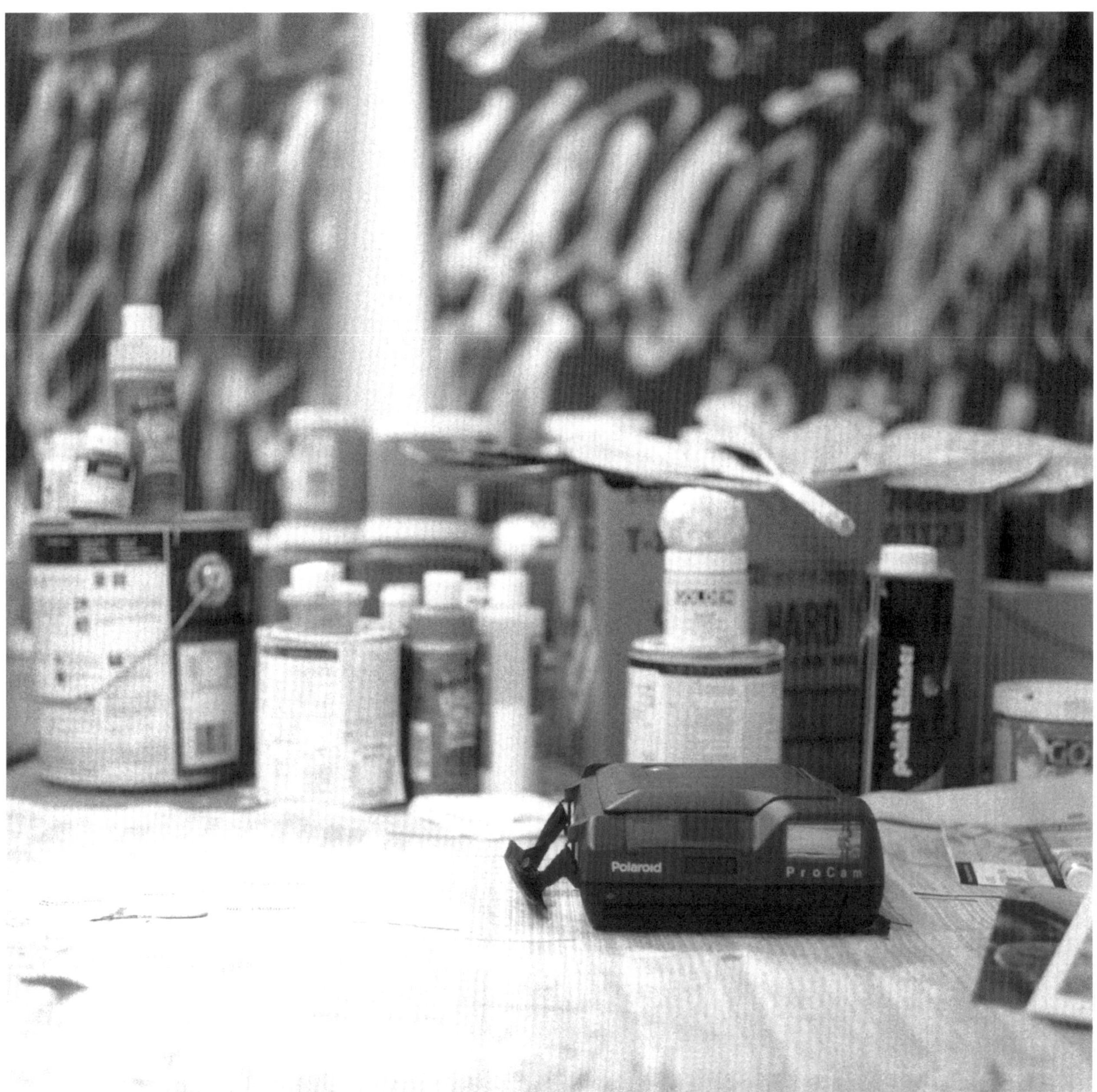
Polaroid
ProCam

MY TIME WITH CY

Rob McDonald

> Every photograph is a certificate of presence. — *Roland Barthes*

For the last twenty years of his life, Cy Twombly returned annually to Lexington, his hometown in the Shenandoah Valley of Virginia. As evidence of his attachment, he bought a house, and during extended visits each spring and fall, he created a number of important works in modest studios he rented in close proximity to downtown. Much of his time here was spent in the company of a small circle of friends. Some of them Cy had known for many years. I was a late addition.

The improbability of coming to know Cy is still a marvel to me. We were introduced in early spring 2002 at a brunch organized by Jean Brown, owner of a local gallery devoted to contemporary photography. Cy's studio was a block away, and he visited the gallery on occasion. One day, I'd been astonished to learn, he purchased one of my photographs, a sepia-toned gelatin silver print depicting the interior of the chapel at Virginia Military Institute in Lexington, where I taught literature. Cy had been intrigued by VMI's antique customs and traditions — many dating from the college's founding in 1839 — since his youth. Jean decided we should meet.

Brunch turned out to be a fitting start because much of our time together was spent over meals. Once or more a week, we'd have breakfast at his favorite diner or supper at my house. We also took long drives, where little was said but much was expressed in his subtle but discernably profound responses to the beautiful countryside of this part of the world.

The place we spent the most time together, however, was Cy's last studio here, at 113 West Nelson Street, a little more than two blocks from his house on Barclay Lane.

Seeing it for the first time, I was taken aback by what a plain space it was, inside and out. The squat, unremarkable building was owned by a local dentist who had used it as his office until his recent retirement. There was a large open front room with a smaller area in back, both lit by fluorescent tubes and furnished with folding tables and white resin chairs likely picked up at Walmart.

But in contrast to such utilitarianism, the place was a visual wonderland reflecting Cy's fondness for gathering and collecting. It was chock-a-block with jars and tubes of paints, bolts of canvas, very many books, and assorted treasures and curiosities picked from yard sales or antique malls—wooden apple boxes, unusual figures and forms, ornate frames varieties of paper ephemera. There were sculptura works sitting about in various states of completion almost as if they'd been left in distraction, but for a just moment. The only spot left relatively free was the interior wall nearest the front door. It would remain clear for long spells, and then one day there'd be panels tacked up, traces of paint skittering across canvas in some new beginning.

Although I photographed inside the studio a number of times, the most sustained view of the space appears in a portfolio of documentary still lifes made in 2007–2008. In those days, I carried my Rolleiflex everywhere, and occasionally I'd ask permission to bring it out. Cy was always present, typically settled into his favorite corner seat, seeming to ignore me as he skimmed the newspaper or peeked through the blinds at passersby. Later, when I showed him the prints, he was drawn to the details, curious about what the camera had picked up.

I never photographed (or ever even witnessed) Cy at work, but once I did inquire about the looping brushstrokes on an untitled series of paintings in deep blue and white underway in the studio at that time. I'd grown obsessed, studying the canvas panels through the camera's viewfinder.

“Do I see letters?” I summoned the courage to ask.

He didn’t even look up from whatever he was reading, but replied with a tone that might have indicated either amusement or intrigue, “Do you?”

The final photographs included here are not from Lexington, but depict the site of Black Mountain College near Asheville, North Carolina. In the summers of 1951 and 1952, Cy and Robert Rauschenberg left New York to study at the now-legendary experimental school, which put studies and practice in the arts at the center of its curriculum.

I’ve had a long-standing fascination with Black Mountain, and one day in October 2009, on a whim while traveling near Asheville, I found what remains of the campus. Lately converted for use as a Christian boys’ camp, the school’s iconic Bauhaus-inspired Studies Building, the main instructional facility, was still standing, and there also was the college’s bucolic centerpiece, Lake Eden. The weather that late fall afternoon was dismal—drizzling rain, low-hanging fog, gray skies—but I was awe-struck.

I decided to call Cy and tell him where I was.

“Are you really?” he asked.

In past conversations, Cy had indulged the occasional question about his time at Black Mountain.

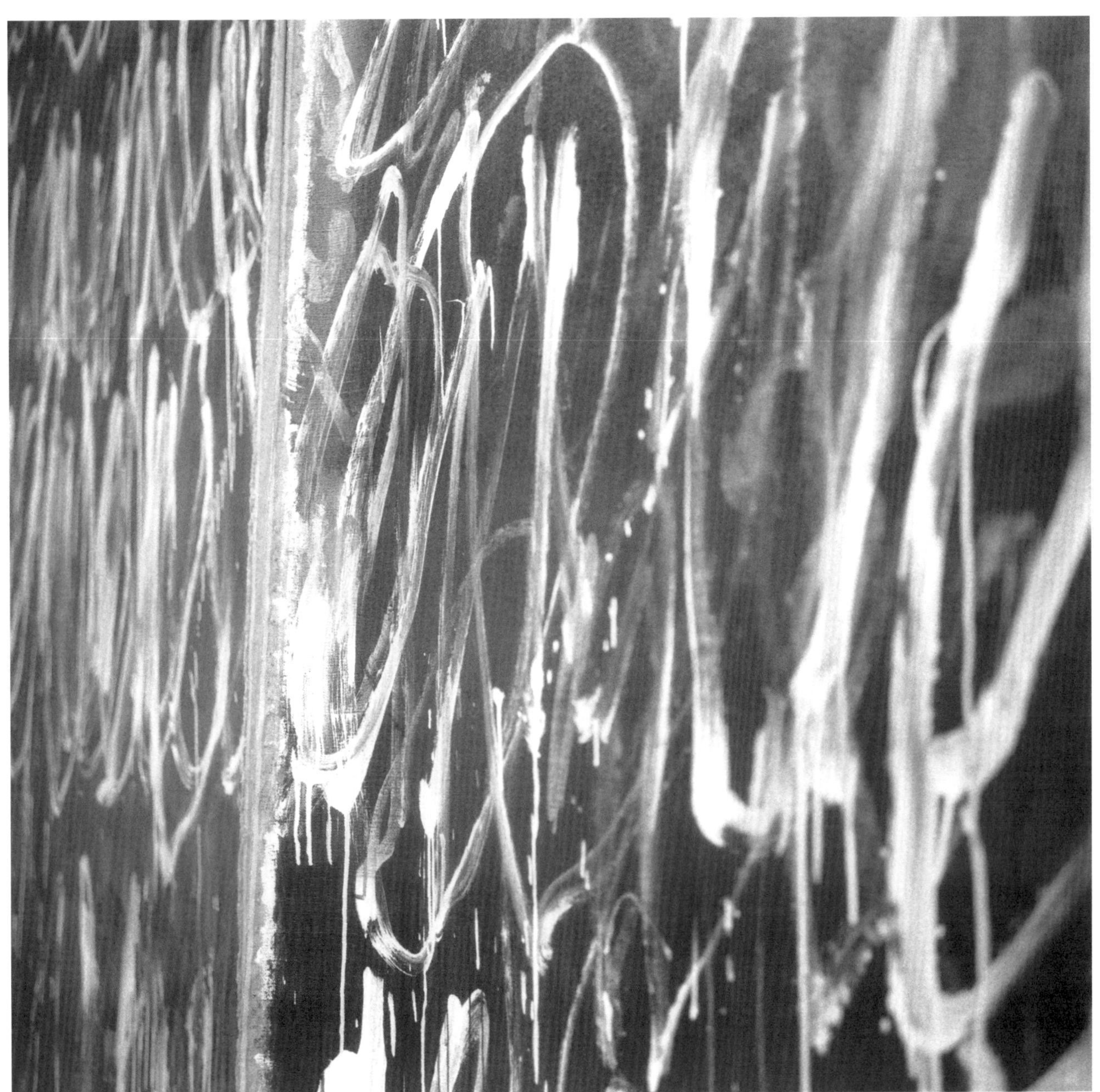

There were many I wanted to ask, but I always deferred to his general preference to talk about the here and now. That afternoon, however, I sensed a churn of interest. His recollection of the place was specific, and he told me about a ground-level room in the Studies Building that he and Rauschenberg had briefly shared as a studio. With him on the line providing directions, I walked straight to the space and shot an entire roll of film, hoping to capture at least the contours of its dim interior, which was lit only by a bank of metal-framed windows.

Most of the negatives from that impromptu visit were underexposed and unprintable, but when I showed Cy the prints I was able to produce, he pored over them as he had the still lifes made in the Nelson Street studio in Lexington. He seemed most interested in the three made inside the Studies Building, the softest images of them all.

He never said, of course, but I have always wondered how those pictures registered against his memories.

I think of that moment now, as I reckon with how all of these photographs, visual notes from our time together, continue to resonate with mine.

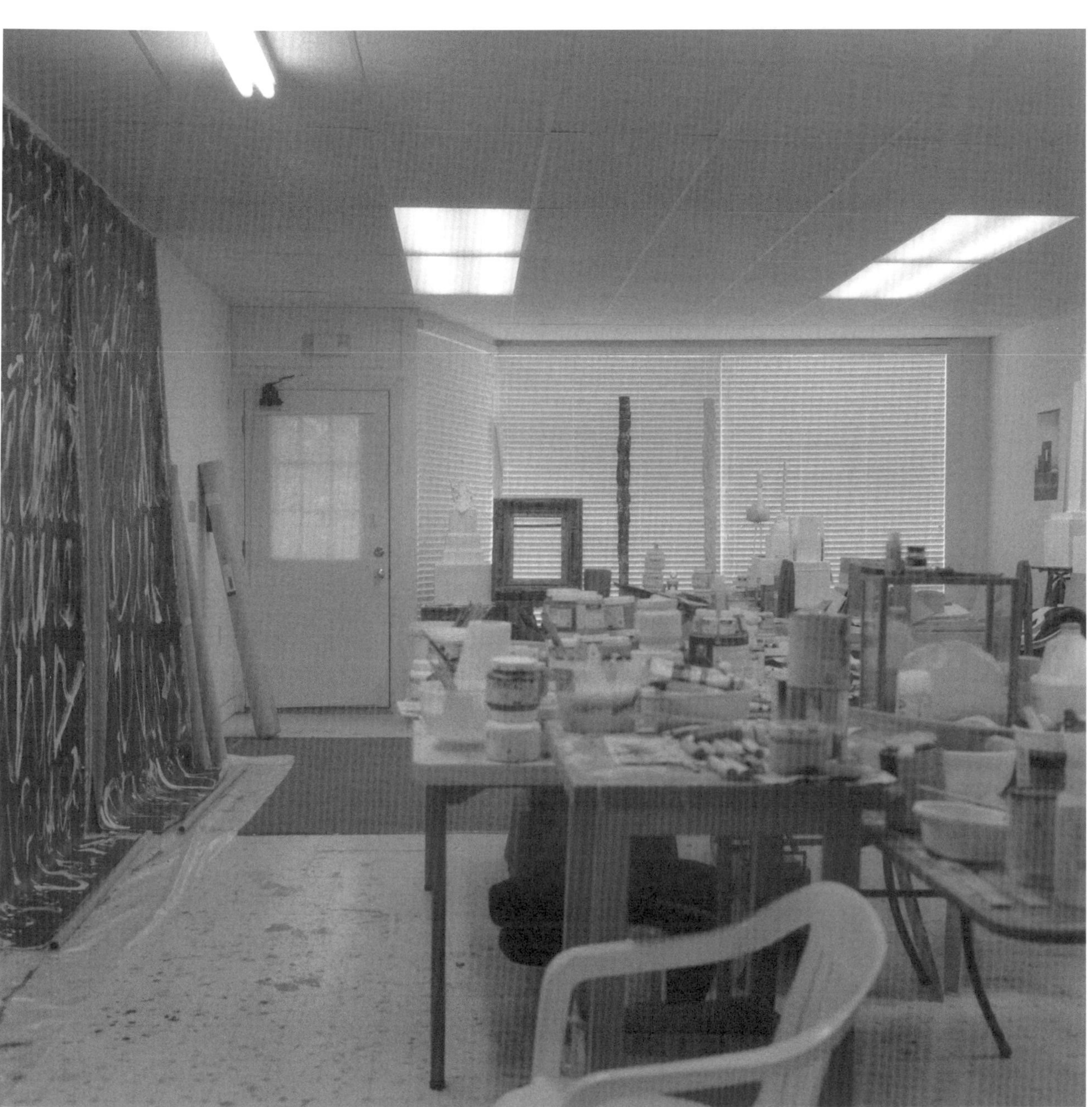

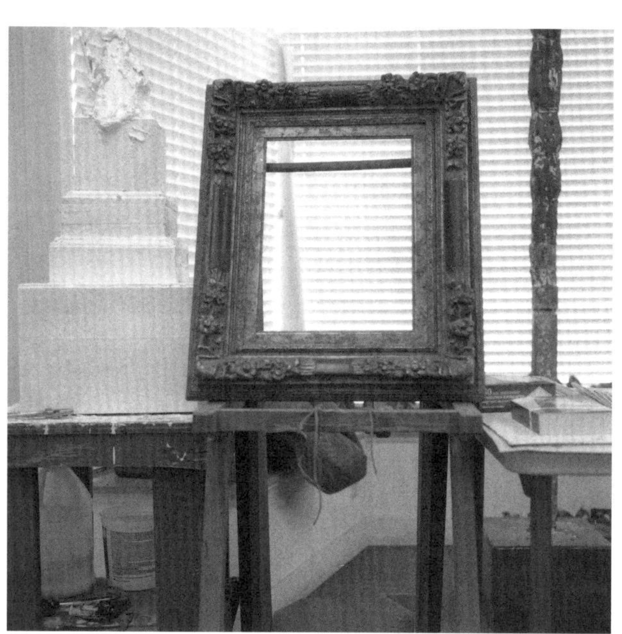

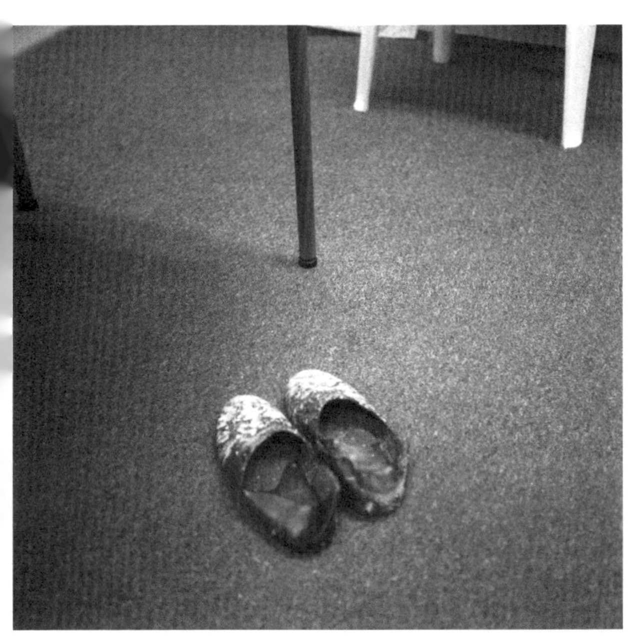

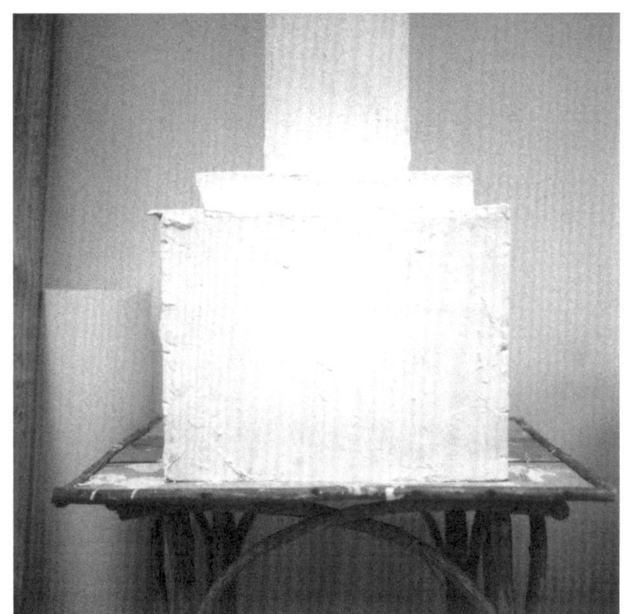

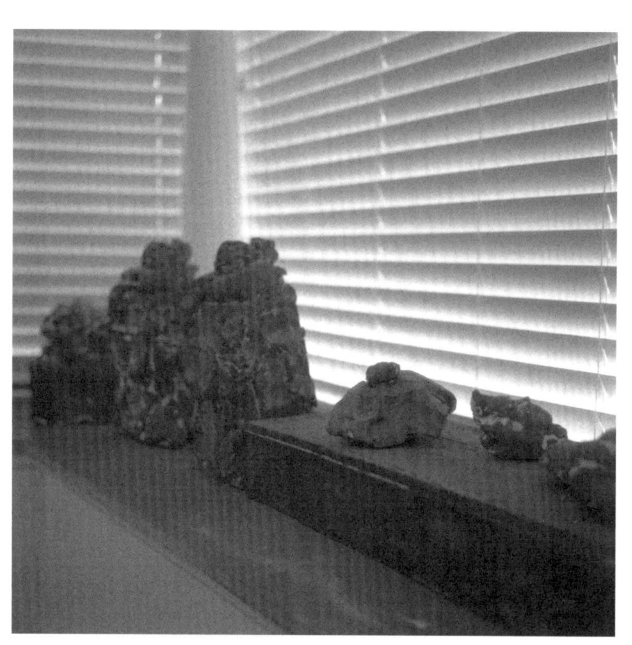

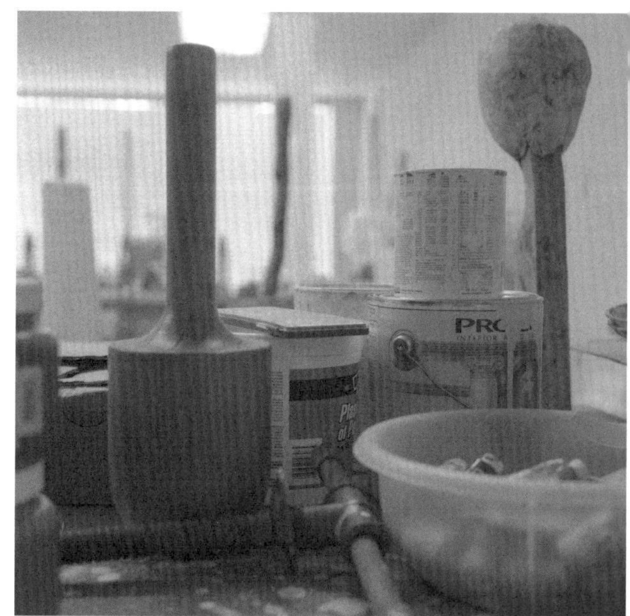

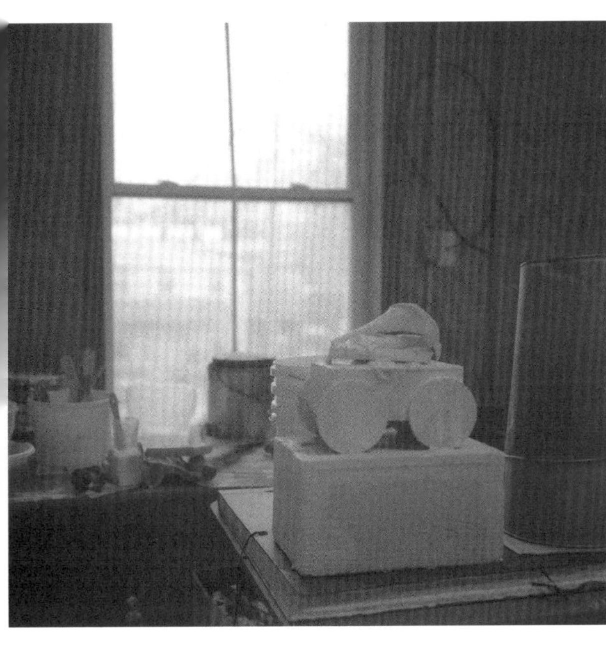

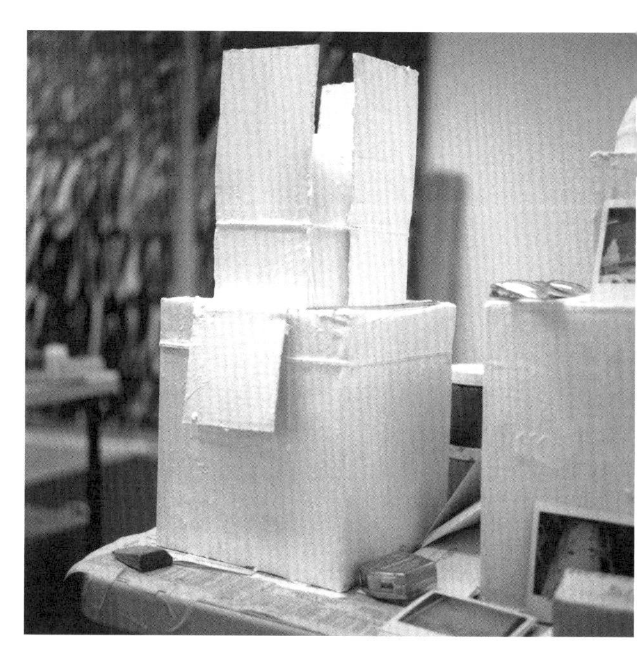

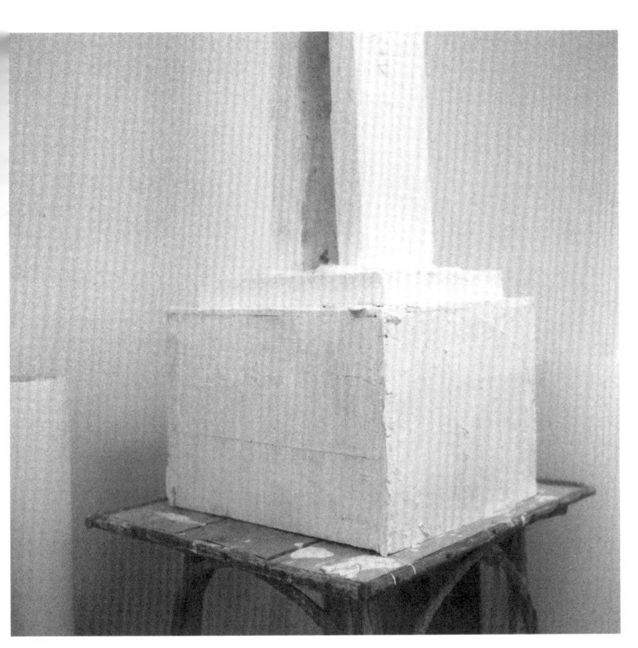

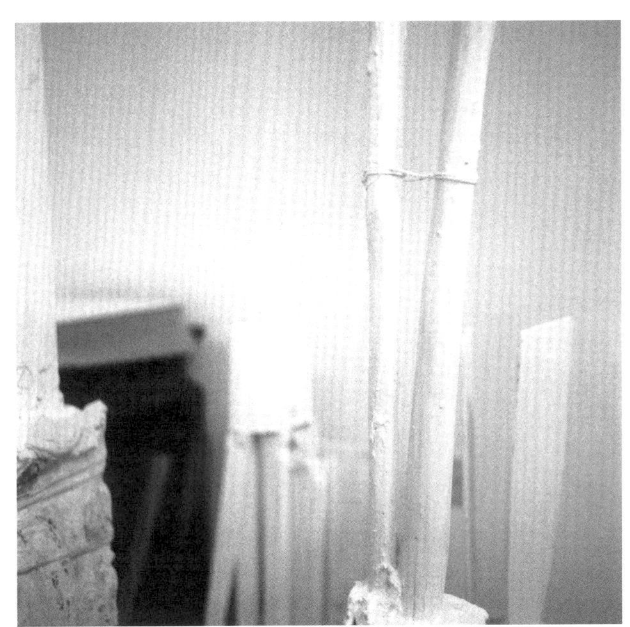

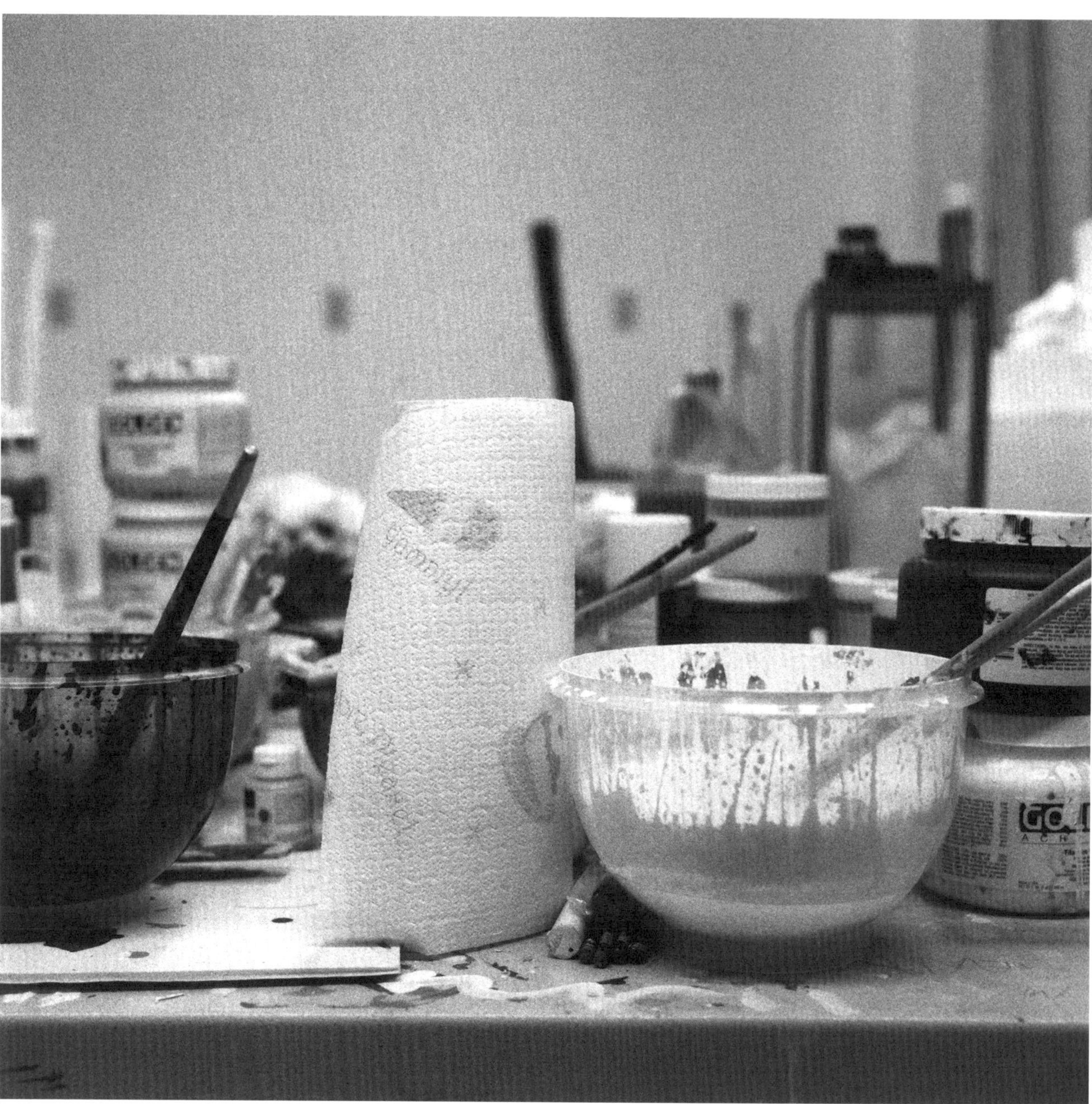

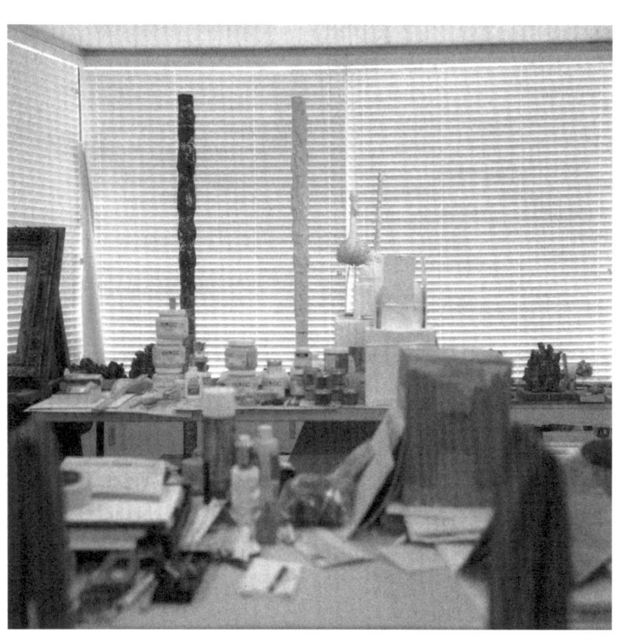

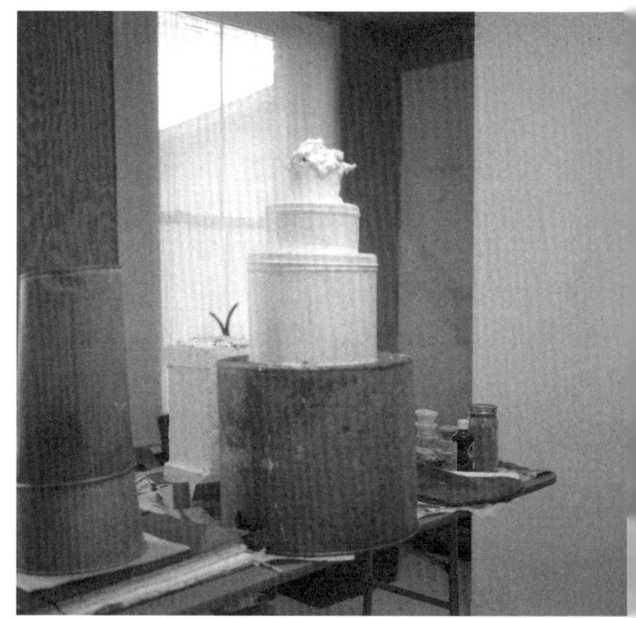

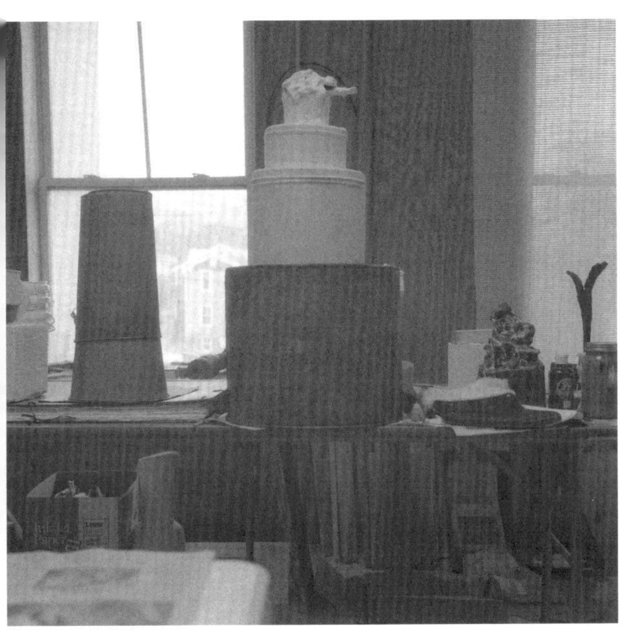

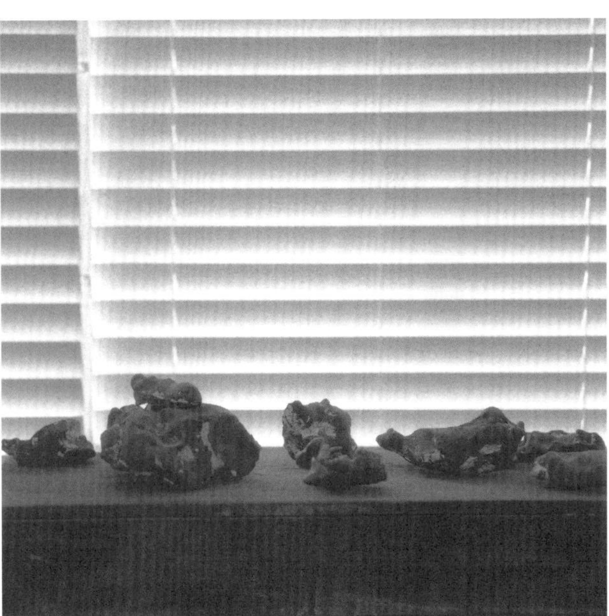

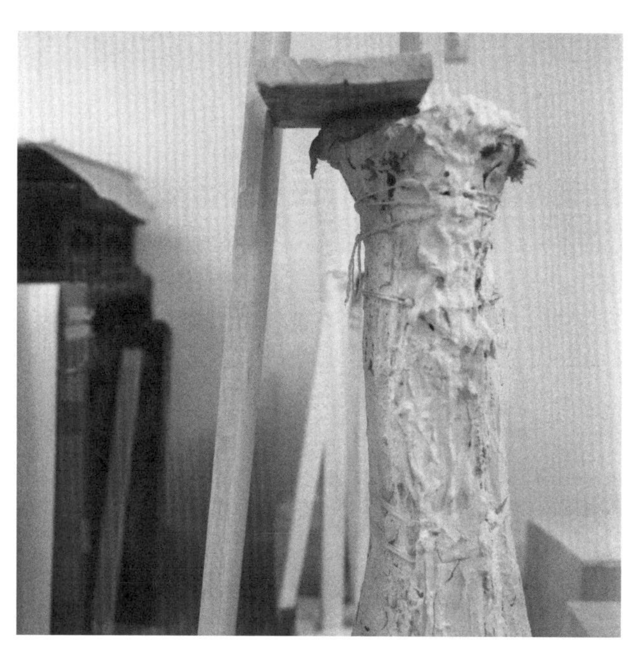

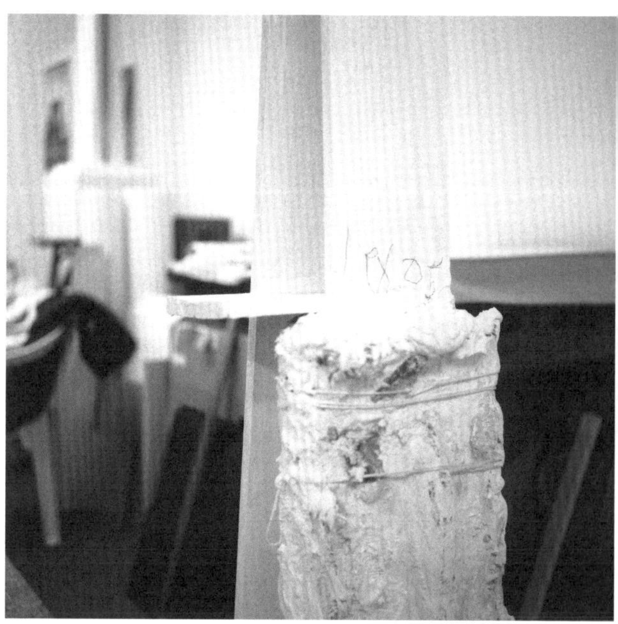

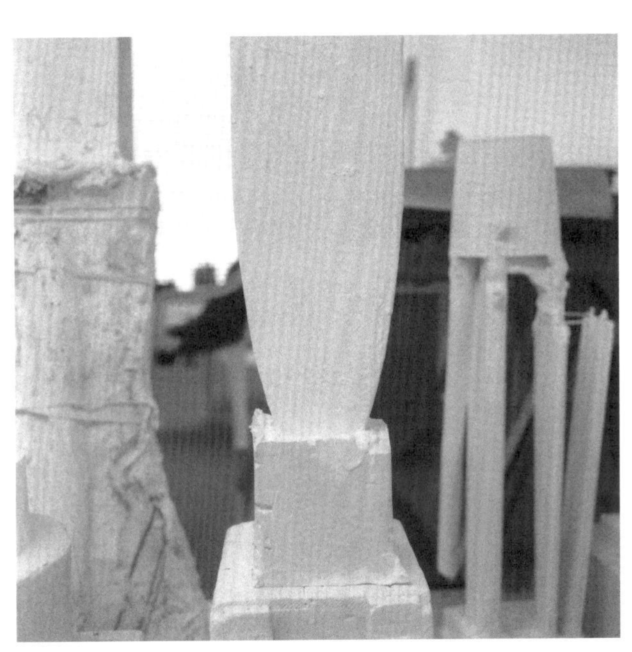

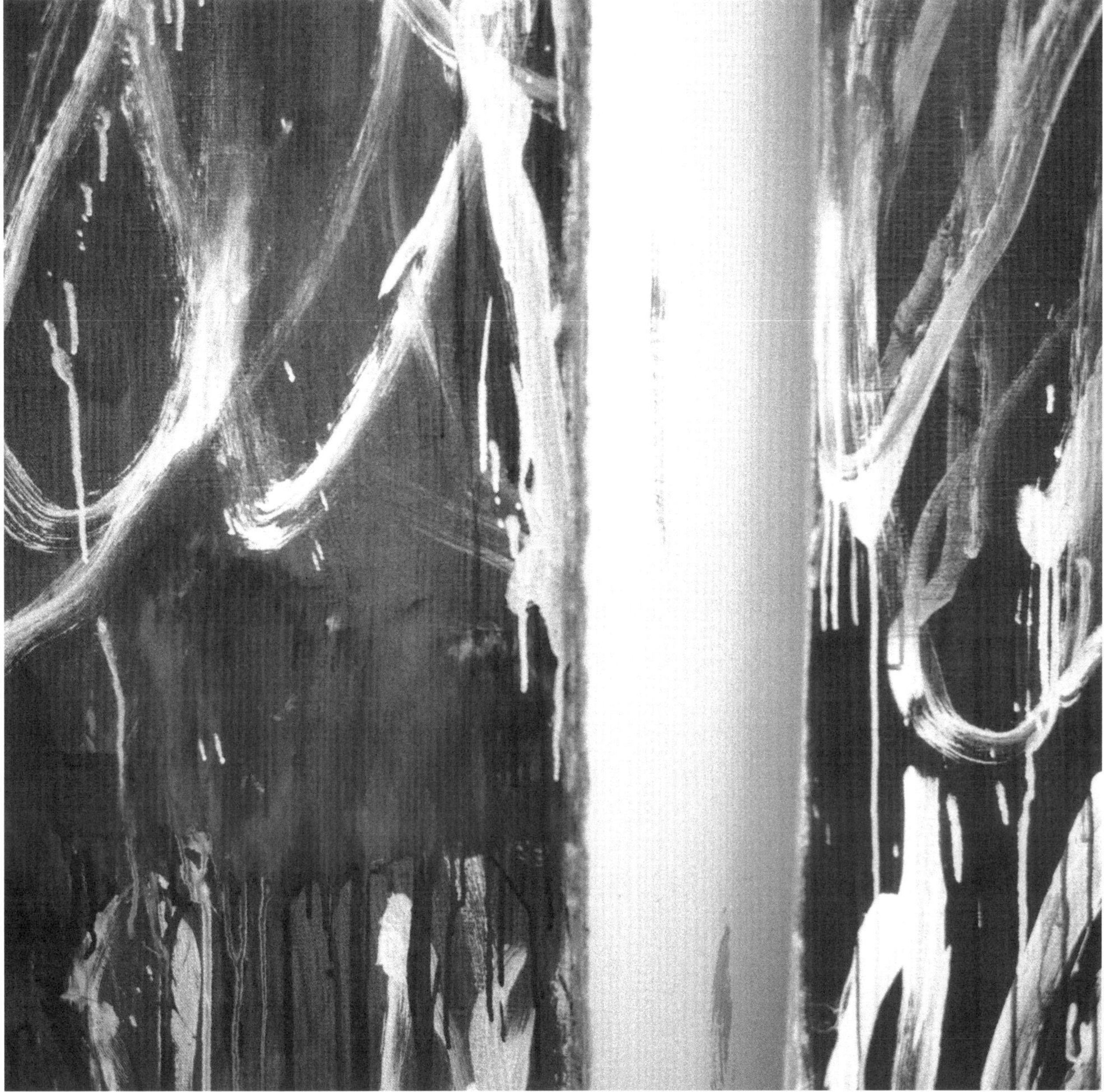

AN ORDINARY STUDIO IN VIRGINIA

Sam Stephenson

In December of 2014, I left my home in Durham, North Carolina, and drove one hundred and eighty miles north into the foothills of the Blue Ridge Mountains, my destination the town of Lexington, Virginia, population just over seven thousand. I was researching the hometown roots of the artist Cy Twombly for an essay that would be published by *The Paris Review*, the literary journal based in New York, in 2015.

The novelist Allan Gurganus, who lives in Hillsborough, North Carolina, encouraged me to reach out to Rob McDonald, a professor of English literature at the Virginia Military Institute in Lexington. Allan had trained as a painter before he became a novelist. Like Twombly, he served as a message decoder in the military as a young man and the two men crossed paths in New York City arts and literary worlds in the 1980s.

Allan told me that McDonald was a close friend of Twombly's during the last decade of the artist's life. He said that Twombly spent half of each year in Lexington, just a few blocks from his childhood home, and during those months each fall and spring he spent time with McDonald and his family. Allan added that McDonald was also a terrific photographer.

It made perfect sense to me that Twombly would befriend a professor of literature. Every book of Twombly's art work contains discussions of his literary influences, from ancient poets to modern, from Ovid, Virgil, Horace, and Catullus to Keats, Eliot, Pound, and Rilke. Many of Twombly's works include phrases, lines, and passages from poems that he scrawled onto his canvases. It also made sense to me that Twombly's literature professor friend in Lexington would also be a visual artist. They originally met after Twombly purchased a few of McDonald's photographs at a local gallery.

Twombly was born in Lexington in 1928. He grew up four blocks from a cemetery which includes the grave of Stonewall Jackson, a general in the Confederate Army during the American Civil War. Confederate General Robert E. Lee is also buried in Lexington. Old Virginian chivalry, grandeur, and discipline are condensed in this tiny mountain cradle. Eighteenth- and nineteenth-century architecture — Greek revival and Queen Anne — prevails in the central part of town. Even the most modest of structures — whether residential, commercial, or institutional — are fronted by venerable columns. When Twombly wandered the gridded blocks from his childhood home toward downtown as a young boy, he must have felt as though he was stepping back in time. It's no wonder that many of the ancient poets he studied were documentarians of tragedy and mythology.

The house Twombly bought in Lexington was just five blocks from his childhood home, on a more regal street even closer to the cemetery where Stonewall Jackson is buried, where both of his parents are buried. He also kept a storefront studio a block away. The second of his two downtown Lexington studios is the one documented by McDonald in this book.

Twombly's parents weren't Southern by birth. They were originally from New England, his mother from Maine, his father from Massachusetts. Cy Sr. took a job in the athletic department at Washington & Lee University in Lexington. The Southern roots quickly went deep for young Cy Jr. In a 1983 interview in W&L's alumni magazine, Twombly said, "It all came from here. All those columns. There are many, many things I never would have done if I'd been born somewhere else."

In a 2007 interview with Sir Nicholas Serota, director of London's Tate Modern, Twombly said, "Virginia made me very Southern in a way. They say that they are not creative in the South, but it's a little rare mentality, it produces writers like a hothouse ...

Faulkner, for example, but also Tennessee Williams and others. It's a literary tradition that I admire, it's totally different from paintings. So in Lexington I always meet professors who hold classes, and someone from Charlottesville (Virginia) said, 'What are you doing, a painter in academia?' I never really separated painting and literature because I've always used reference."

McDonald was born and raised in South Carolina, giving him more that he shared with Twombly, roots in the South and a twang in his voice. McDonald's kids grew up knowing "Mr. Twombly," not aware that he was one of the most famous painters in the elite end of the global art world.

The British artist and filmmaker, Tacita Dean, who is based in Berlin, visited Twombly in Lexington in 2011, just nine months before his death. She made a subtle and sublime twenty-nine-minute film from her visit, simply showing Twombly going about a normal day in town, sorting mail, reading an article in *The Financial Times* about his New York gallery owner, Larry Gagosian, making comments about a new biography of Keats, eating at his favorite local diner where everyone knew him. She titled it *Edwin Parker*, Twombly's legal first and middle names, given by his parents. In an essay accompanying the

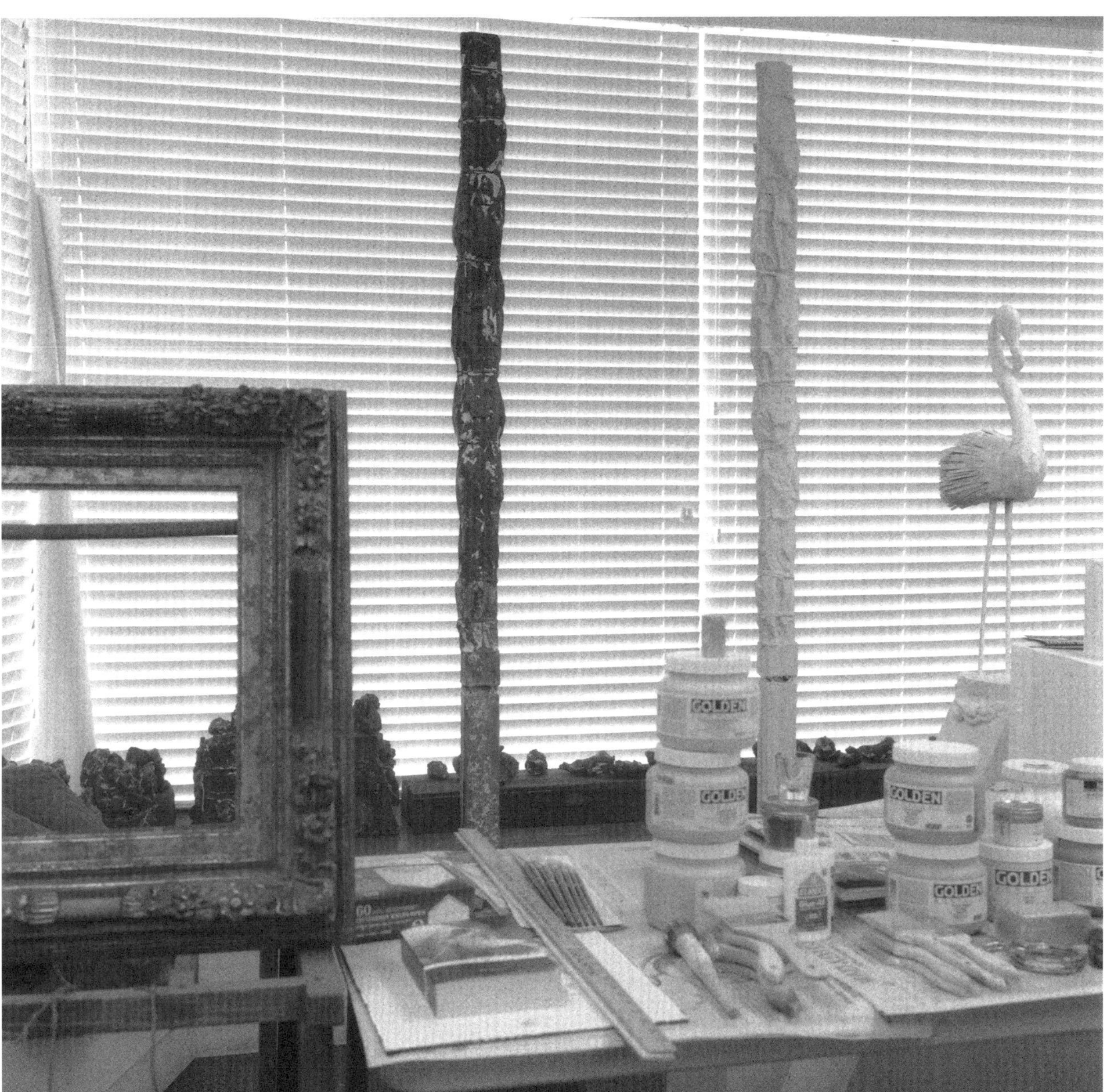
GOLDEN
GOLDEN
GOLDEN
GOLDEN
GOLDEN

film, she wrote, "For Cy, painting is pure behavior and that's why he doesn't talk about it. I asked him if he worked in spurts and he replied that he wasn't 'nine to five.' He is an artist blessed with pictorial instinct and with a true ability to work beneath his conscious level, and that is rare. Much of his working time is spent getting to his point. There is no preparation, or rather his preparation is sedentary, spent reading and reflecting and being."

When Twombly received a DVD of Dean's completed film later in 2011 he took it over to McDonald's house for viewing. Twombly didn't have a DVD player. He knew that McDonald's family did. He seemed to admire the film as he watched it but when it was over the only thing he said, turning to McDonald, was, "That's what I look like?"

I met McDonald for lunch at a grill in downtown Lexington. Introduced from afar by Allan Gurganus we immediately had much common ground. I was eager to learn about his friendship with Twombly. Among many other things, McDonald told me about one of his routines with Twombly. On Friday afternoons, he accompanied Twombly on visits to the military parade ground on the campus of the Virginia Military Institute. Twombly's longtime studio and personal assistant in Lexington, Butch Bryant a local middle-aged man, drove them to the same corner of the ground. If McDonald was already on campus, he would make the short walk from his office to meet Twombly and Bryant. The three of them would sit together in the car, or McDonald would bring folding chairs if the weather was especially good. Twombly gazed westward, over the organized, fluid movements of the marching cadets, toward House Mountain which rose about eight miles outside of town.

After lunch McDonald and I walked to this corner of the parade ground. He told me, "Cy said, many times, that he'd been all over the world, but the VMI parade ground—surrounded by all this neo-Gothic architecture, including the barracks, and with House Mountain in the distance—was near the top of the most beautiful places he knew. It was hard for me to process that, but he clearly meant it."

In McDonald's photographs of Twombly's studio in Lexington, and in Tacita Dean's film, the blinds on the former storefront windows appear. A retail store was in this space when Twombly was a kid. The sidewalks that Twombly walked daily as a kid laid just beyond the windows. Some of these pieces of concrete would have the same disjunctions as they did decades ago, corners pushed up an inch or two by relentless tree roots, or sunk by four seasons of distinct weather year after year. There is a lazy flow of automobile traffic outside, daily deliveries recognizable by distinctive truck sounds.

Twombly's studio was so far away, geographically and metaphorically, from Gagosian's gallery, or MoMA, or the Tate Modern, or fill in the blank with the most rarefied centers of modern art in the world. It was ordinary. McDonald's quiet photographs, as with Dean's subtle film, remind us that extraordinary things can happen in these places that are otherwise forgotten.

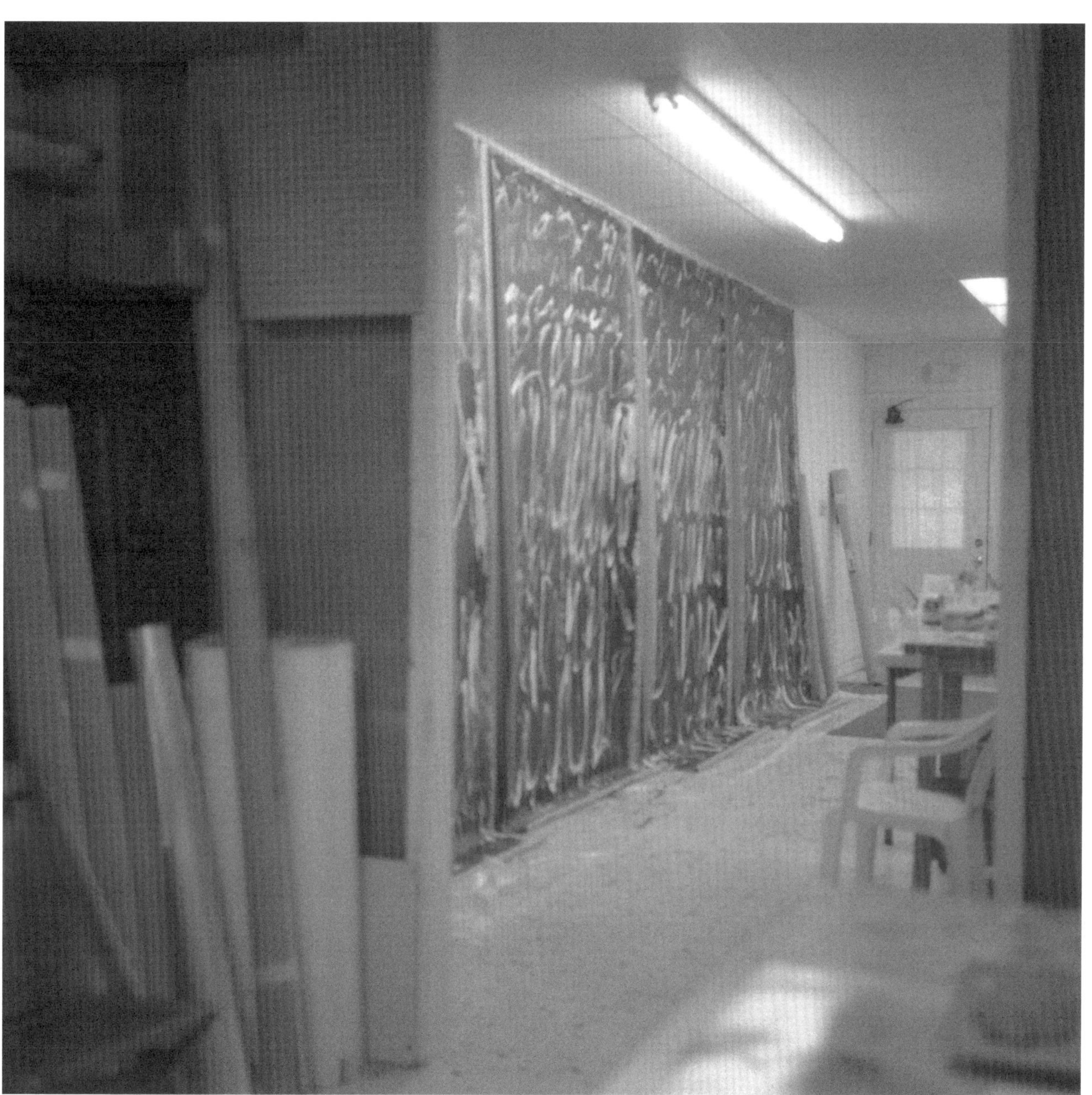

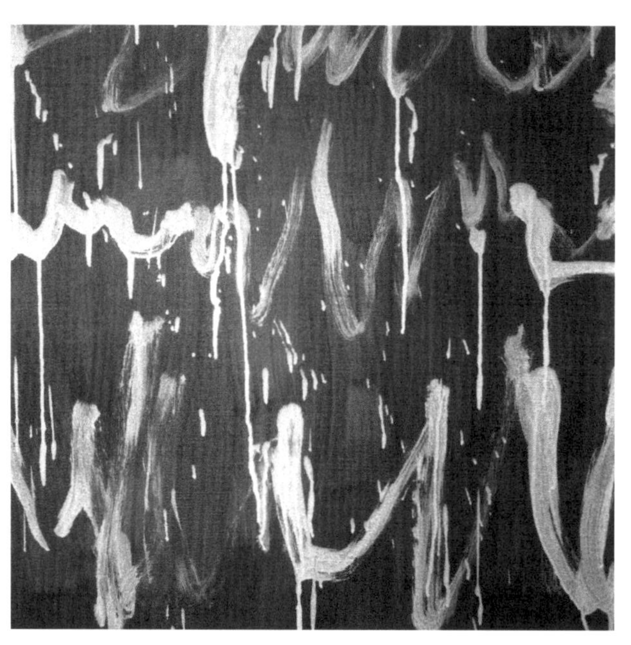

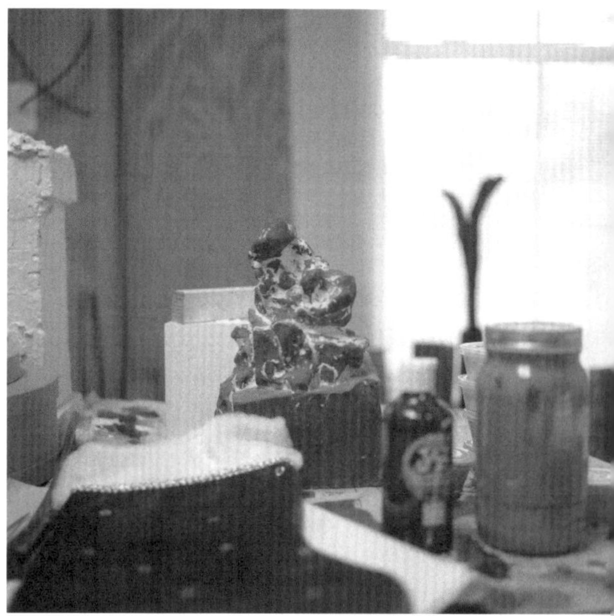

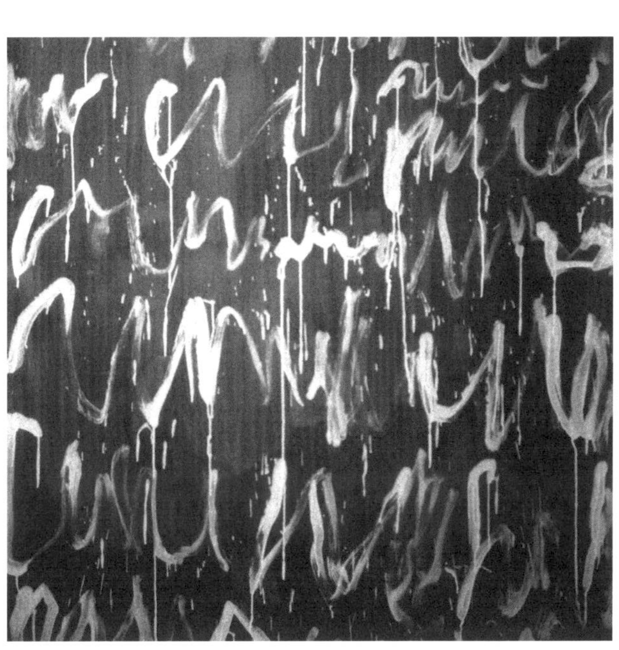

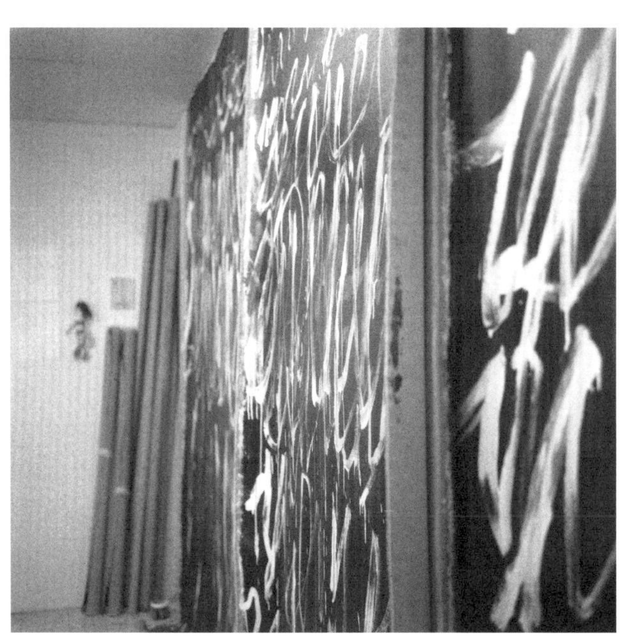

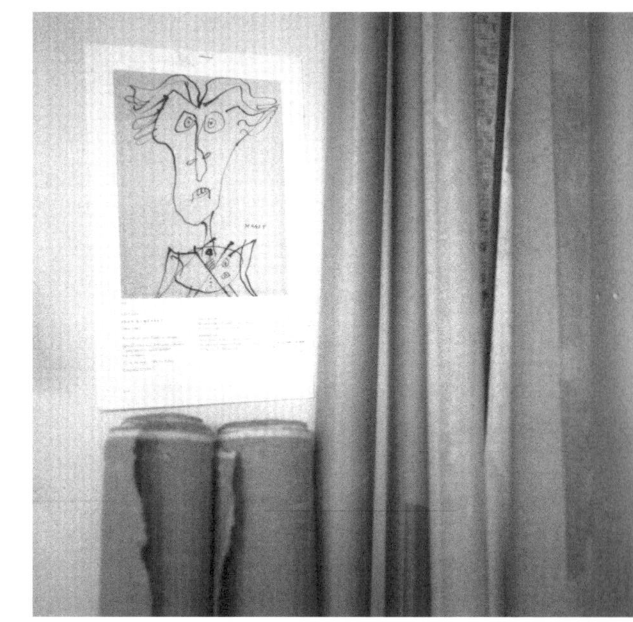

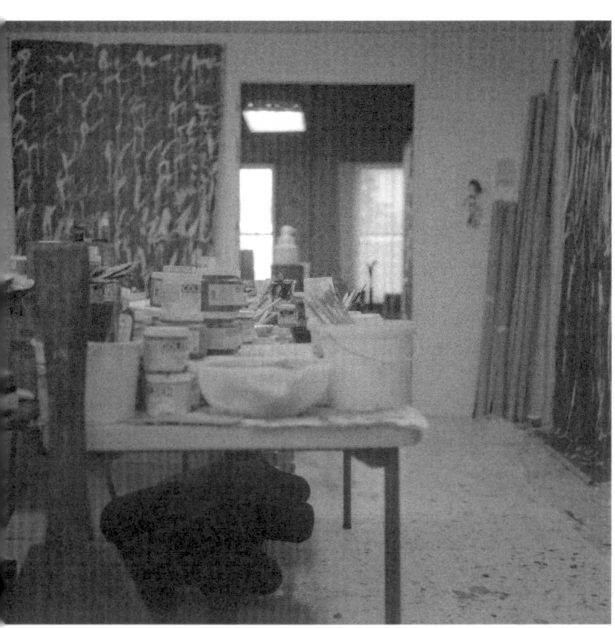

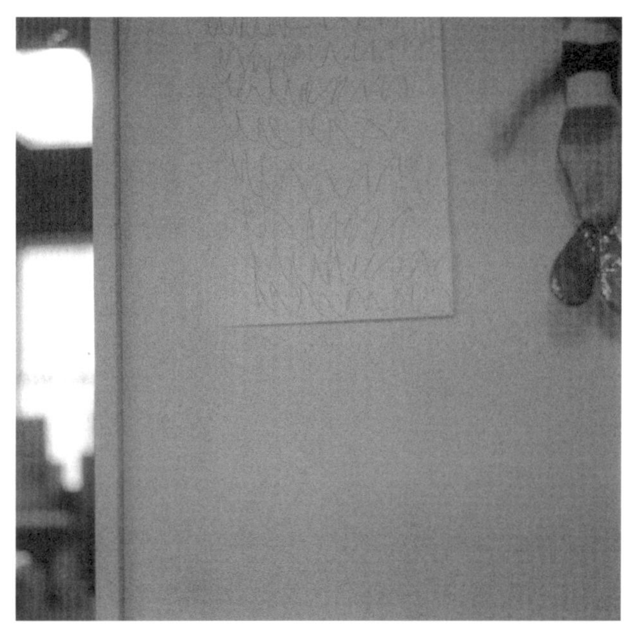

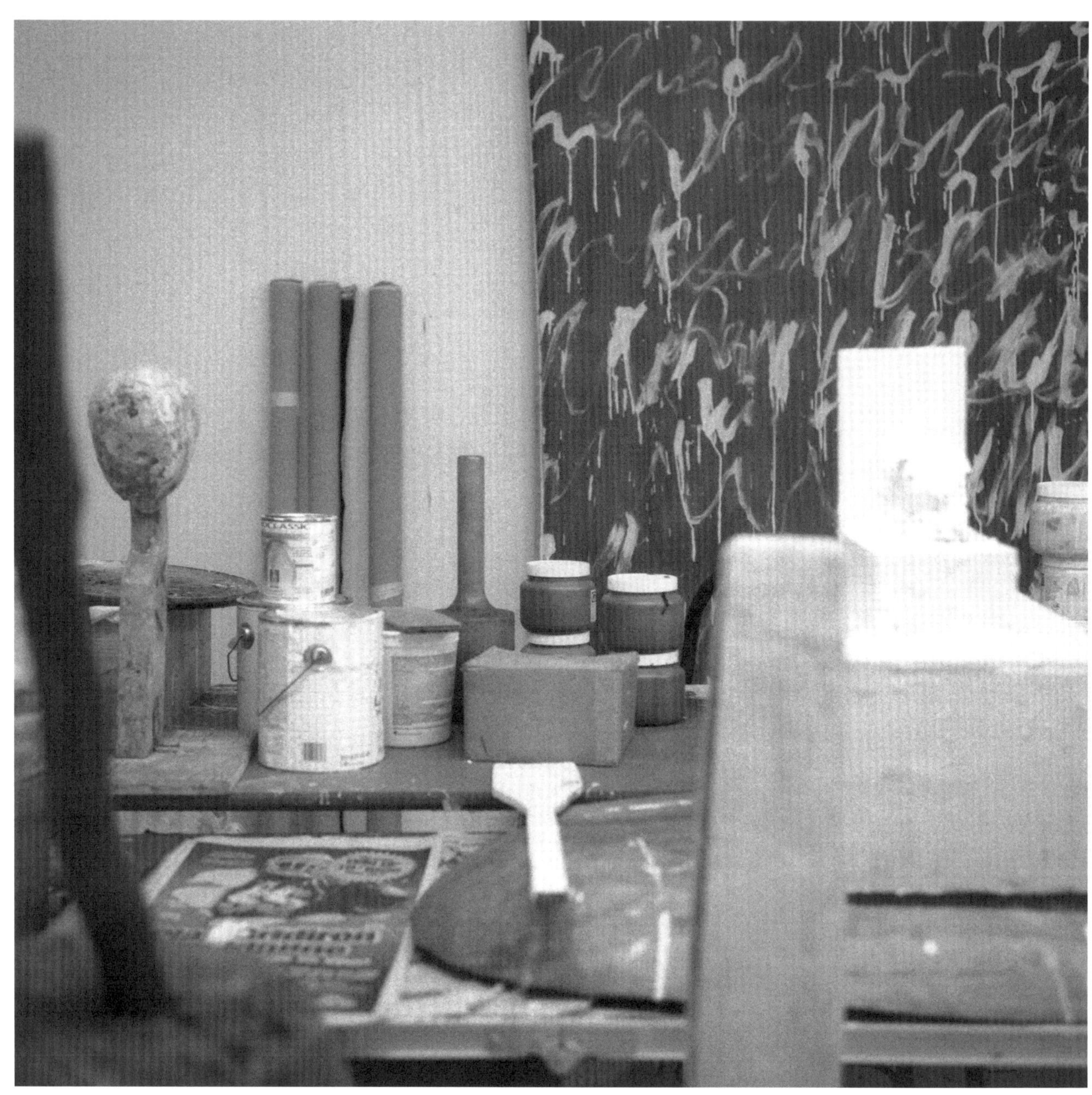

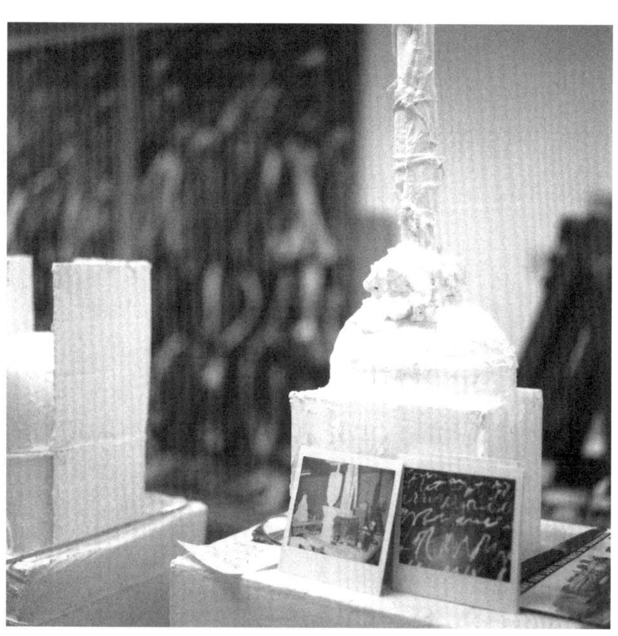

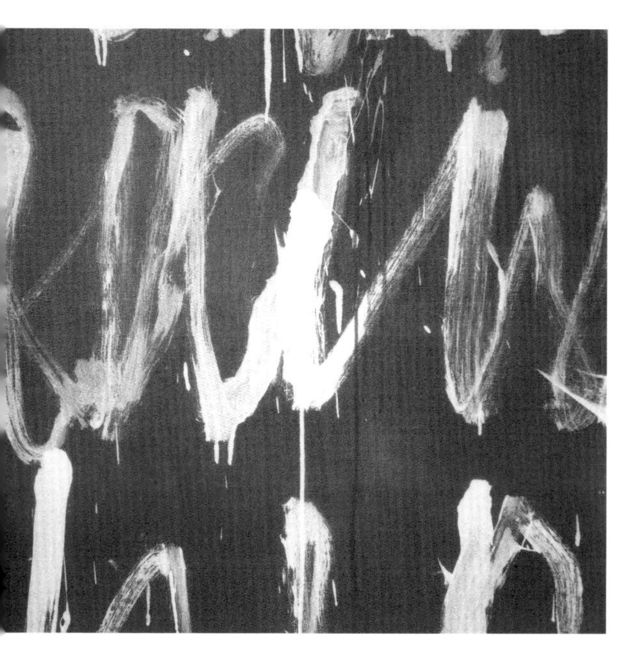

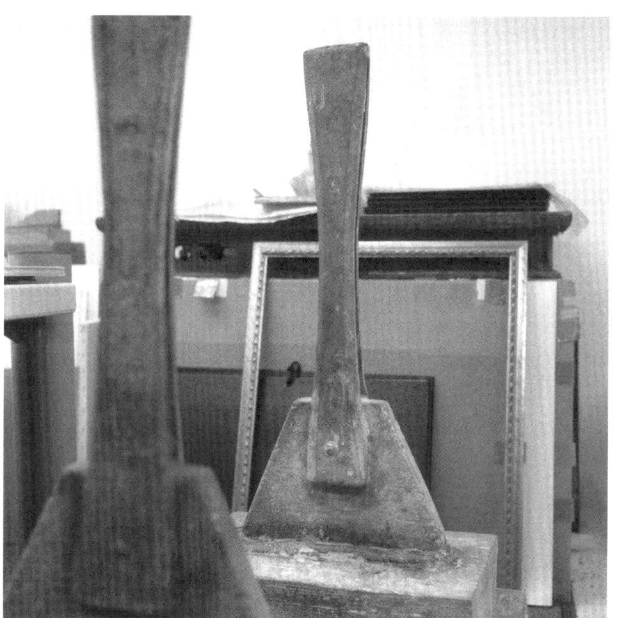

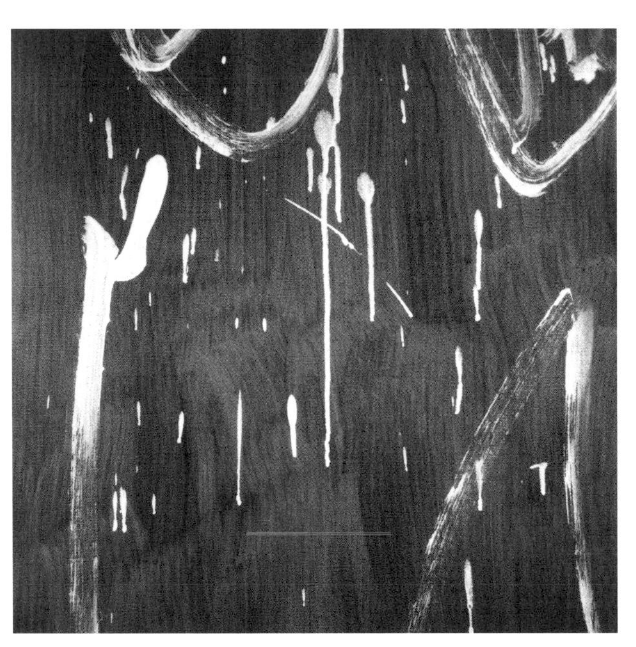

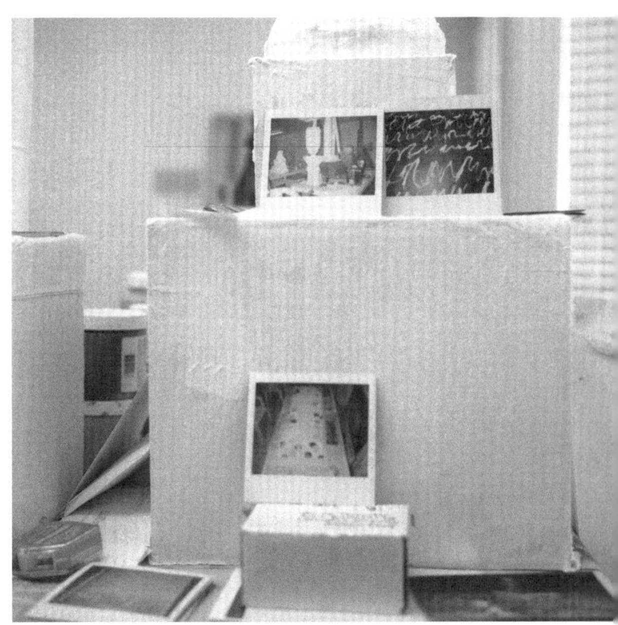

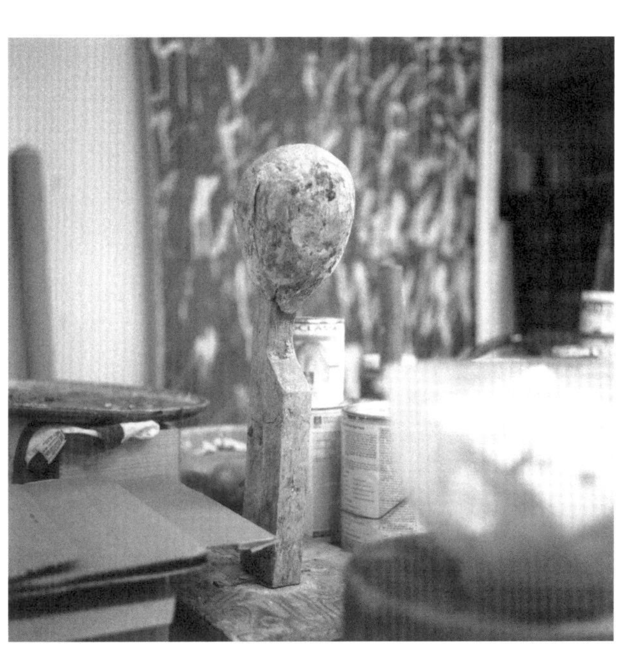

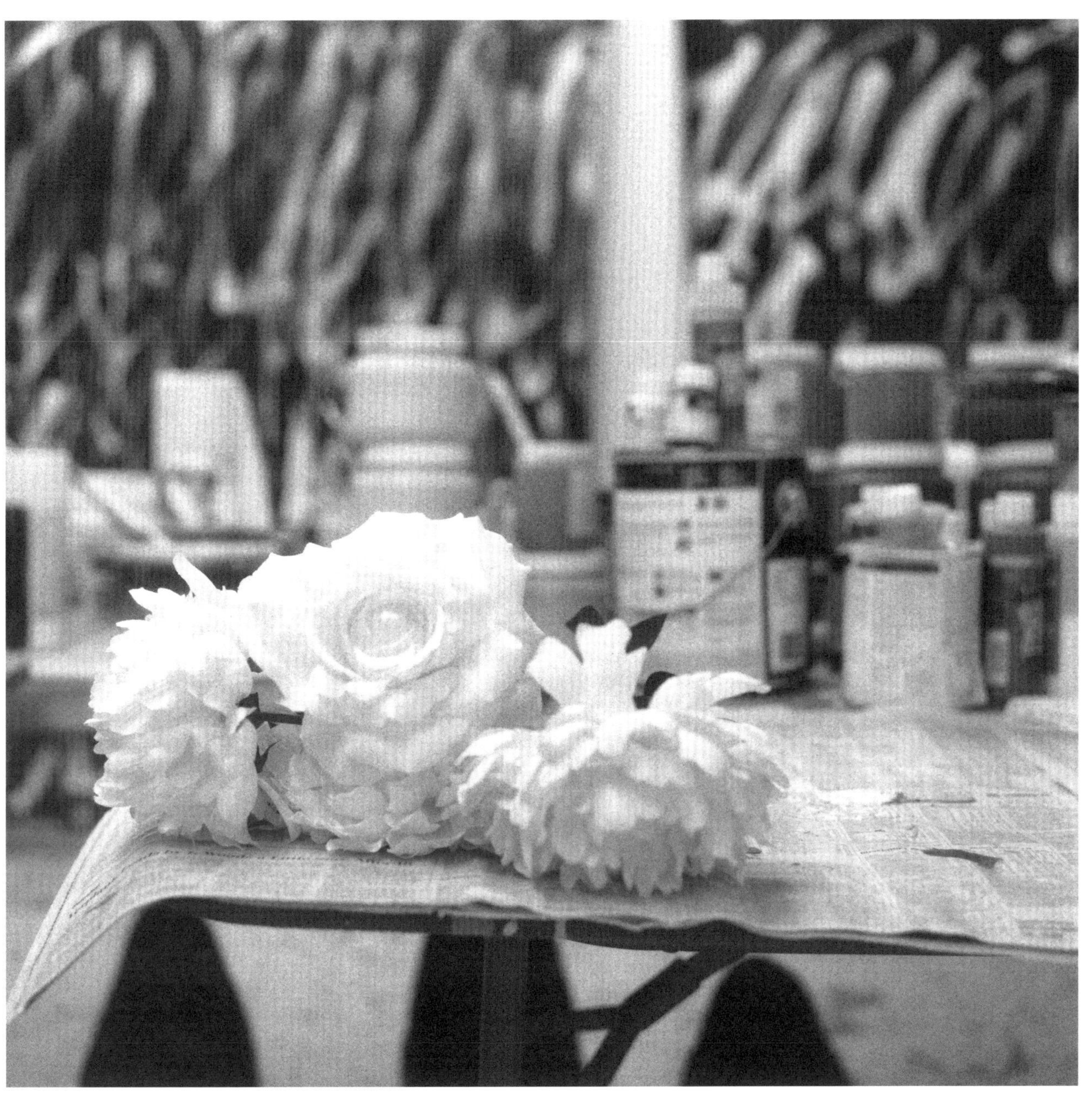

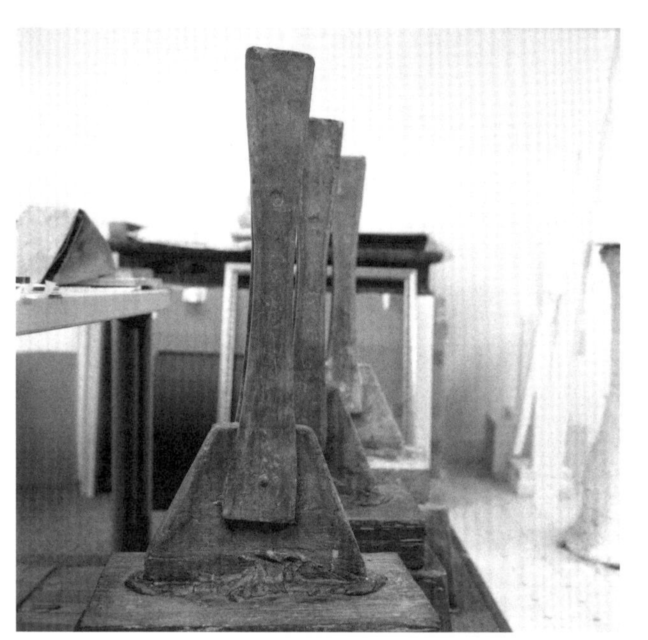

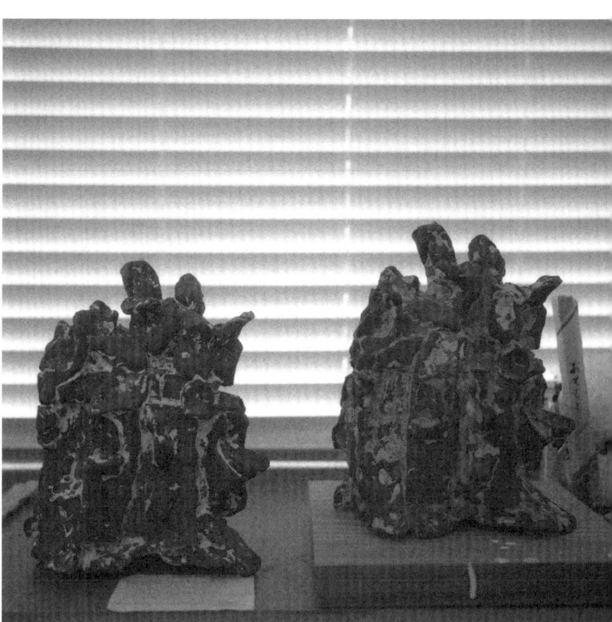

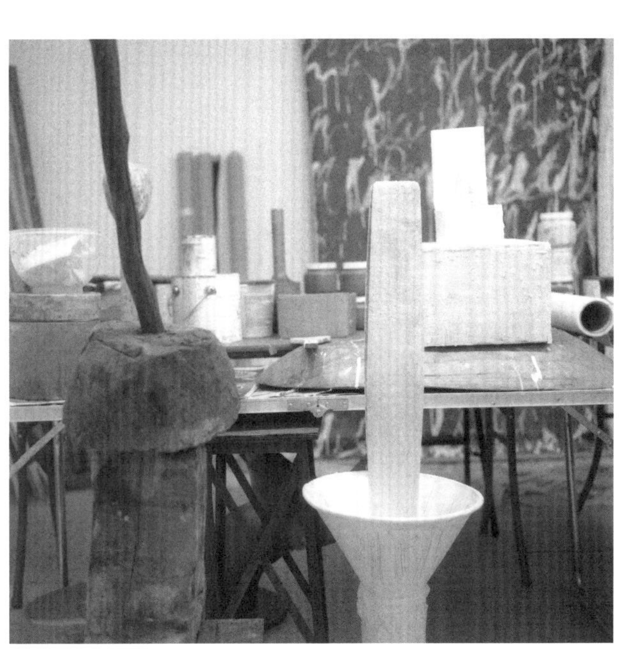

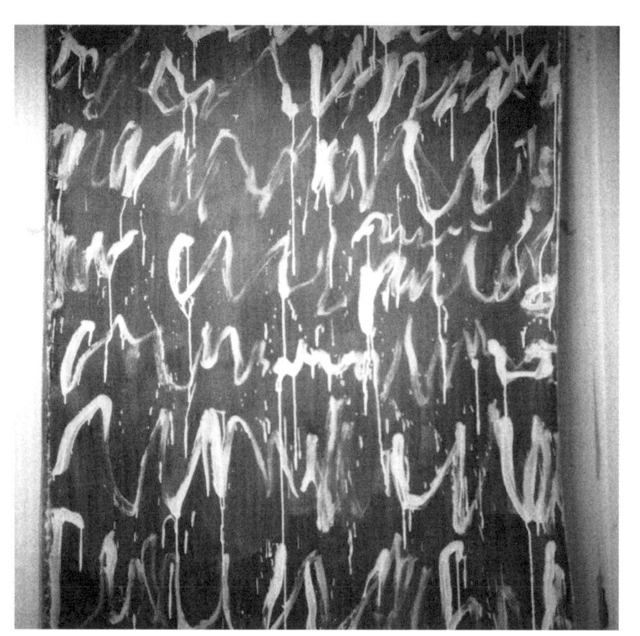

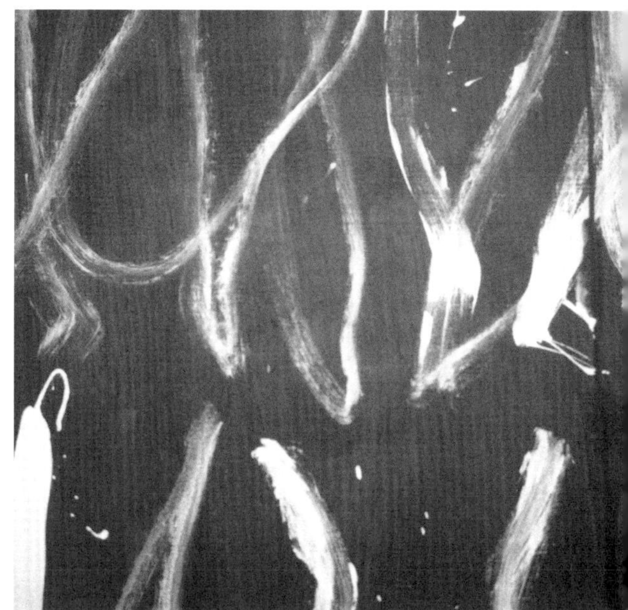

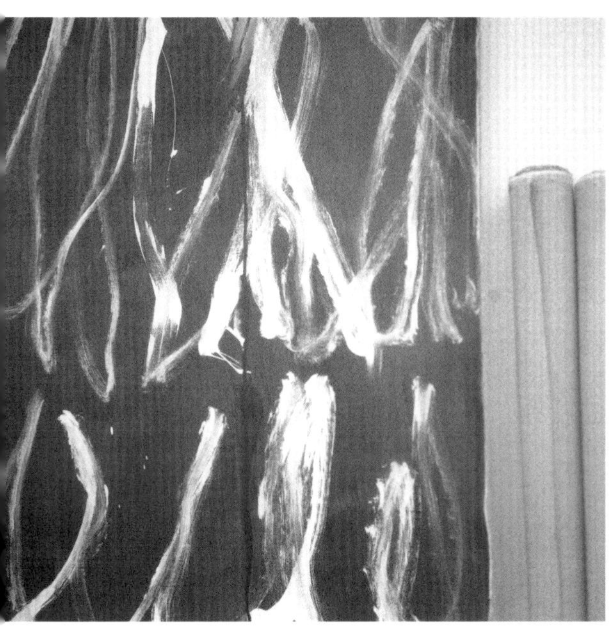

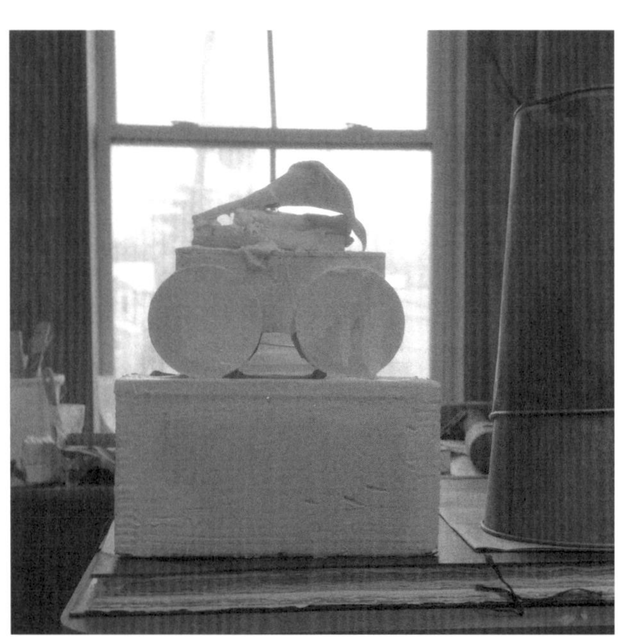

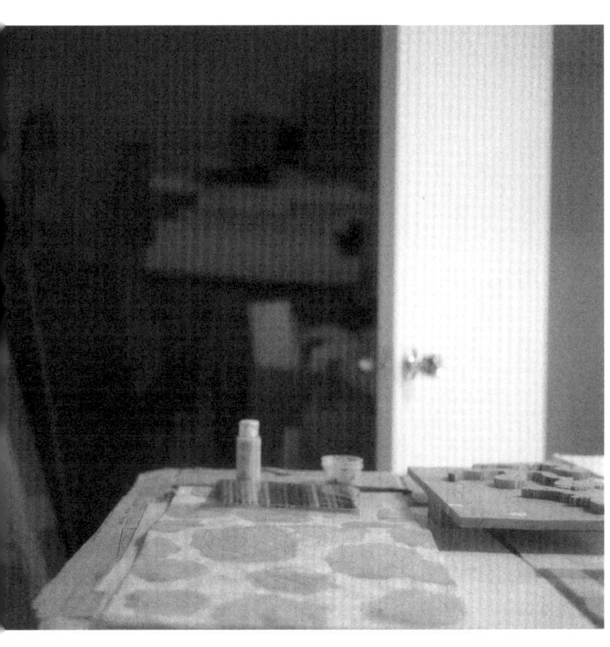

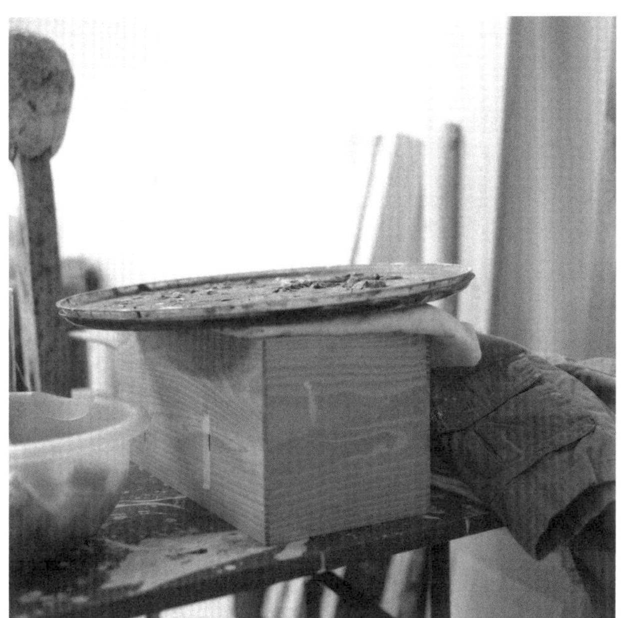

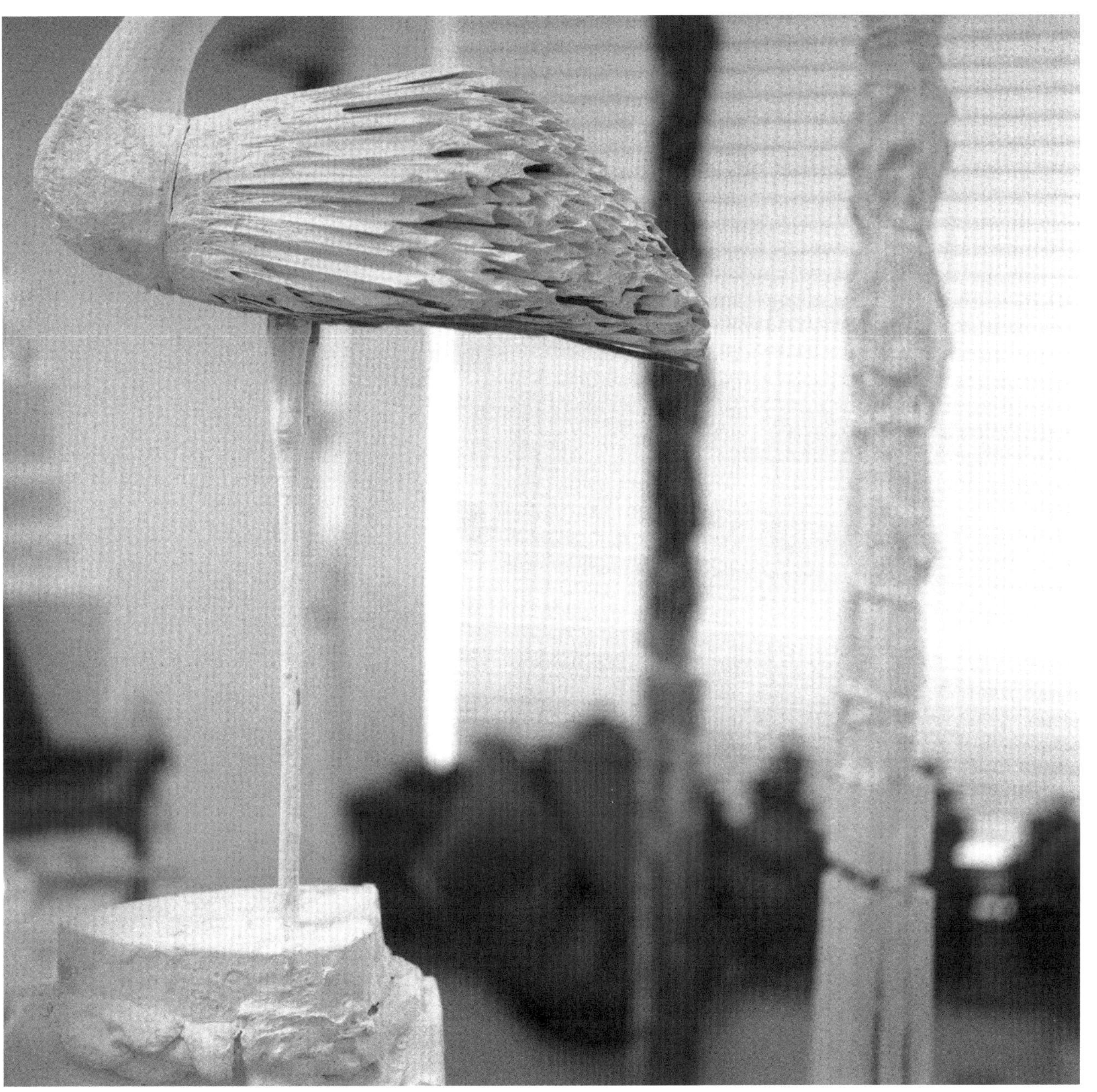

"DRAWN TO THE DETAILS": ROB MCDONALD AND CY TWOMBLY

Thierry Greub

In *The Pencil of Nature* (1844) William Henry Fox Talbot wrote of his photographic study *The Open Door*, which shows a broom of twigs leaning on a weatherbeaten doorway, "A painter's eye will often be arrested where ordinary people see nothing remarkable. [...] A casual gleam of sunshine, or a shadow thrown across his path, a time-withered oak, or a moss-covered stone may awaken a train of thoughts and feelings, and picturesque imaginings."

The photographic works of Rob McDonald set in motion just such a "train of thoughts and feelings." His photo-essay *Native Ground* (2014) looks at the living spaces of famous Southern writers to gauge the importance of place in the process by which a writer's imagination takes form, and he writes of it: "*Native Ground* is an ode to [...] writers and the places that inspire in them the words for things that matter. The photographs are documentary only insofar as they begin in attention to particular writers' personal spaces and native landscapes. What interests me most is how the images can suggest resonance, how places inhabited might be imagined to shape vision and voice."

This eliciting of imaginative resonances and associative "picturesque imaginings" through personal living spaces and landscapes brings into focus essential elements of Rob McDonald's photographic works. It was a picture in the *Native Ground* series that moved Cy Twombly to have Rob McDonald photograph his studio. The artist, originally from Lexington, Virginia, had spent several months in his hometown every year since his "return" from Italy in 1993. In the ten years before his death, Twombly and the literary scholar and photo-artist McDonald enjoyed an intense friendship.

Rob McDonald's *Studio Notes* went on show for the first time in 2023 in the AnzenbergerGallery in Vienna. They consist of several series of images, both in color and in black and white, taken at various times in the context of his friendship with Cy Twombly. The present volume comprises two black-and-white series: the pictures of Cy Twombly's last studio in Lexington, under the title *Studio Still Lifes* (2007/08), and the 2009 series *Black Mountain College*. The latter series shows, among other things, the workspace shared by Twombly with Robert Rauschenberg as an art student in 1951/52 at this legendary educational institution.

The personal character of these pictures is invoked by the subtitle of *Studio Notes*: "My time with Cy." They came about as a visual equivalent of a diary, a kind of personal exploration and record of the Lexington studio space in which, according to McDonald, Twombly truly "lived," whereas at his house he seemed as if he were only visiting.

Before Rob McDonald, a series of leading (photographic) artists had caught glimpses of Twombly's changing workplaces and homes in New York, Rome, Bassano in Teverina, Gaeta, Itri, and Lexington, as can be seen in the illustrated volume published in 2019 by Nicola Del Roscio and Florian Illies, *Cy Twombly: Homes & Studios*. Over a period of fifty years of creative working, these places were captured in photographs by, among others, Robert Rauschenberg, Cy Twombly's wife, the painter and photographer Tatiana Franchetti-Twombly, Horst P. Horst, Ugo Mulas, Annabelle d'Huart, Deborah Turbeville, Bruce Weber, François Hallard, David Seidner, Sally Mann, Tacita Dean, and, not least, Cy Twombly.

A "portrait" of Cy Twombly's last Lexington studio on West Nelson Street was produced in 2011 in a film by Tacita Dean and, before her, by Sally Mann in several series of photographs from 1999 to 2012. Mann's works were exhibited with Gagosian and published in 2016 in a book of photographs, *Remembered Light:*

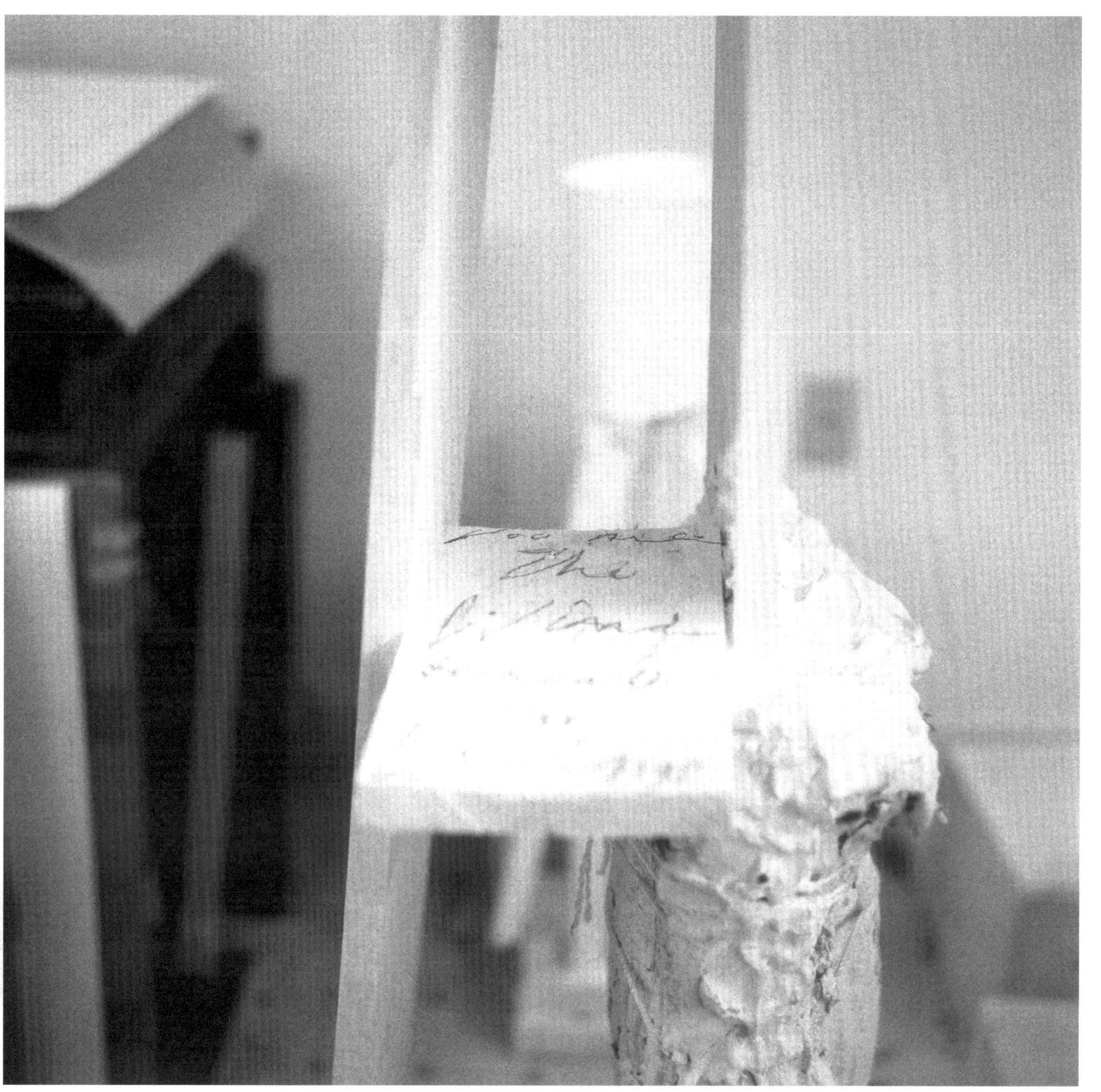

Cy Twombly in Lexington. In her autobiography *Hold Still* (2015) she recounts how she had known this friend and artistic mentor since her teenage years.

In Sally Mann's photographs, the real protagonist of the pictures is the light. In dazzling contre-jour it dissolves the contours of objects or, seeping indirectly through lowered blinds, it paints patterns and abstract forms on floors and walls. Sally Mann's studies of interiors charge Twombly's studio space with an aura as the site of luminous epiphanies. In contrast, Tacita Dean's 30-minute film *Edwin Parker* (the artist's birth-name) strips the aura from Twombly's studio: it is a place where the octogenarian sits in his favorite corner before the large front window, browses a Keats biography, looks at Polaroids, and finally drives off with Nicola Del Roscio and his assistant to a nearby diner.

An artist's studio is a macrocosm in itself. It is both a space for physical action and at the same time a space for reflection, in which the artistic idea takes concrete form. For Twombly, an essential element of artistic-creative practice consisted of "periods of thought." In 1991 a photograph by Deborah Turbeville captured one such moment in the artist's palazzo in Bassano in Teverina: he sits in an armchair and waits, surrounded only by empty canvases hanging on the studio walls. Twombly recounted that he mostly took a long time to reach the "state of mind" that made the creative act possible—a state of "fusing of ideas, fusing of feelings, fusing projected on atmosphere." On the process—difficult to communicate, highly emotional but at the same time extremely physical—by which the artistic imagination took form, he said: "It's not the focus. It goes beyond. It's something else where everything runs together. If you're in that state all the time you'd be dizzy, you'd fall down."

Twombly would let this emotional arousal flow through him until it built up into an inner charge, which was discharged in an eruptive act of painting. "He seemed to work with such [...] an energy that almost burst out of him and into the canvas," is how Sally Mann describes his radically embodied way of working. Each viewer of the artworks of Cy Twombly will experience this emotional energy in an individual way. The intensity of the stimulus that acted on the artist is transferred to the viewer as a "residual energy." For this Twombly used a concept from physics, "remanence," to refer to a state of excitement that remains after a stimulus. The excitements that stimulated artworks in this way were set in motion, for Twombly, by emotional experiences, or works of art, but also by literary fragments, or the impressions made by landscapes.

Central to Twombly's concept of art was the pursuit of "the ultimate essence even if it is 'contaminated.'" In order to capture this "ultimate essence" of the subject, it needs to be freed from "contaminations" in the form of earlier stages of reception and layers of interpretation. This becomes all the more difficult the better known a given picture's theme is, and hence the more loaded its content has become.

For Rob McDonald, approaching one of Cy Twombly's studios meant addressing a motif that was overloaded with the impressions of earlier images by renowned colleagues. In his photograph of the artist's paint-spattered work shoes, he was also picking up a theme that has been powerfully promoted as a metaphor in art theory, namely the artist's shoes (one need think only of the texts by Martin Heidegger, Meyer Schapiro, or Jacques Derrida on Van Gogh's shoes). Cy Twombly himself had in 2002 photographed the slippers he wore while painting, flecked in yellow and white. His Polaroid image shows them at extreme close range, so the motif is still just recognizable, but is transformed to

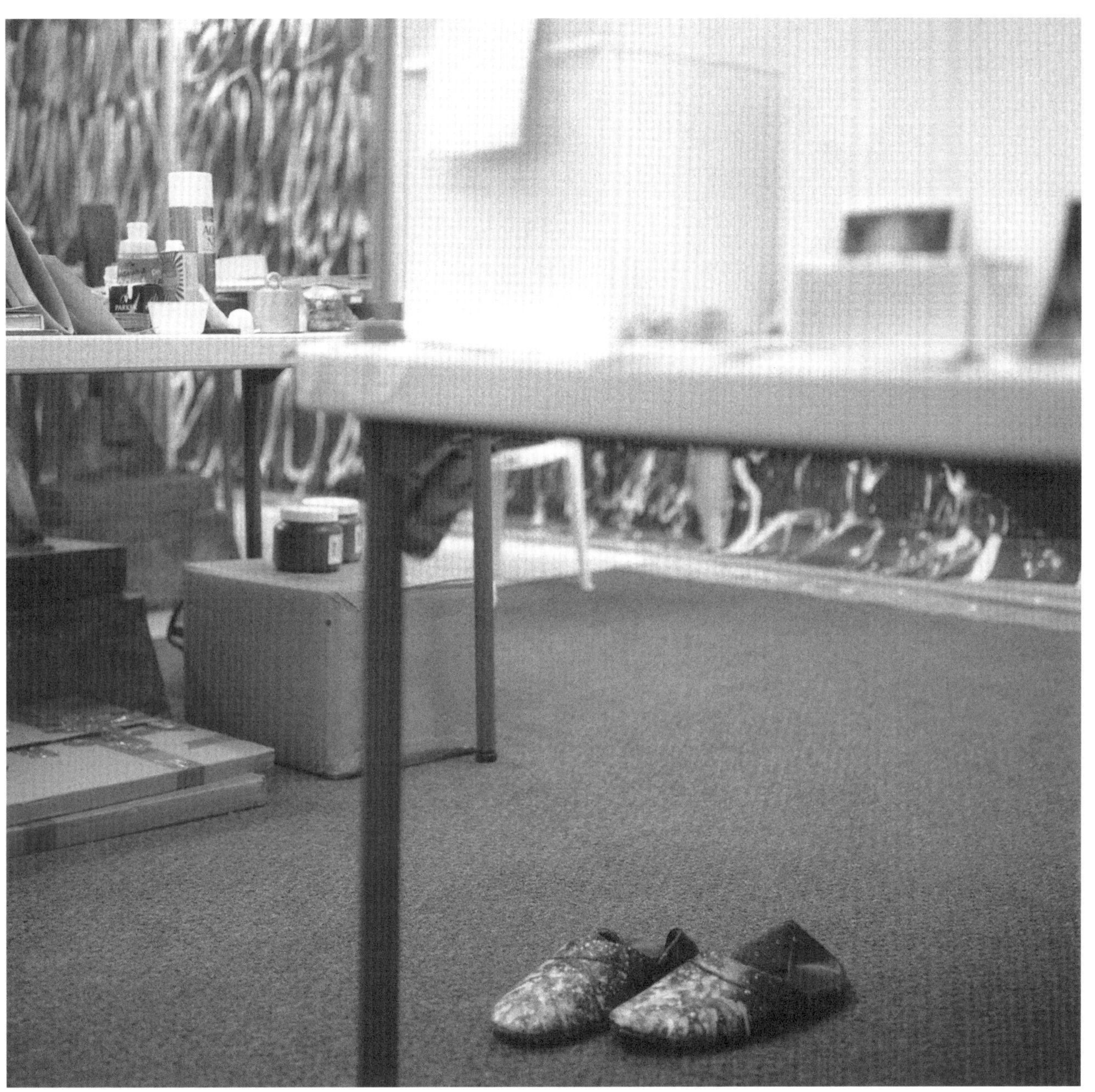

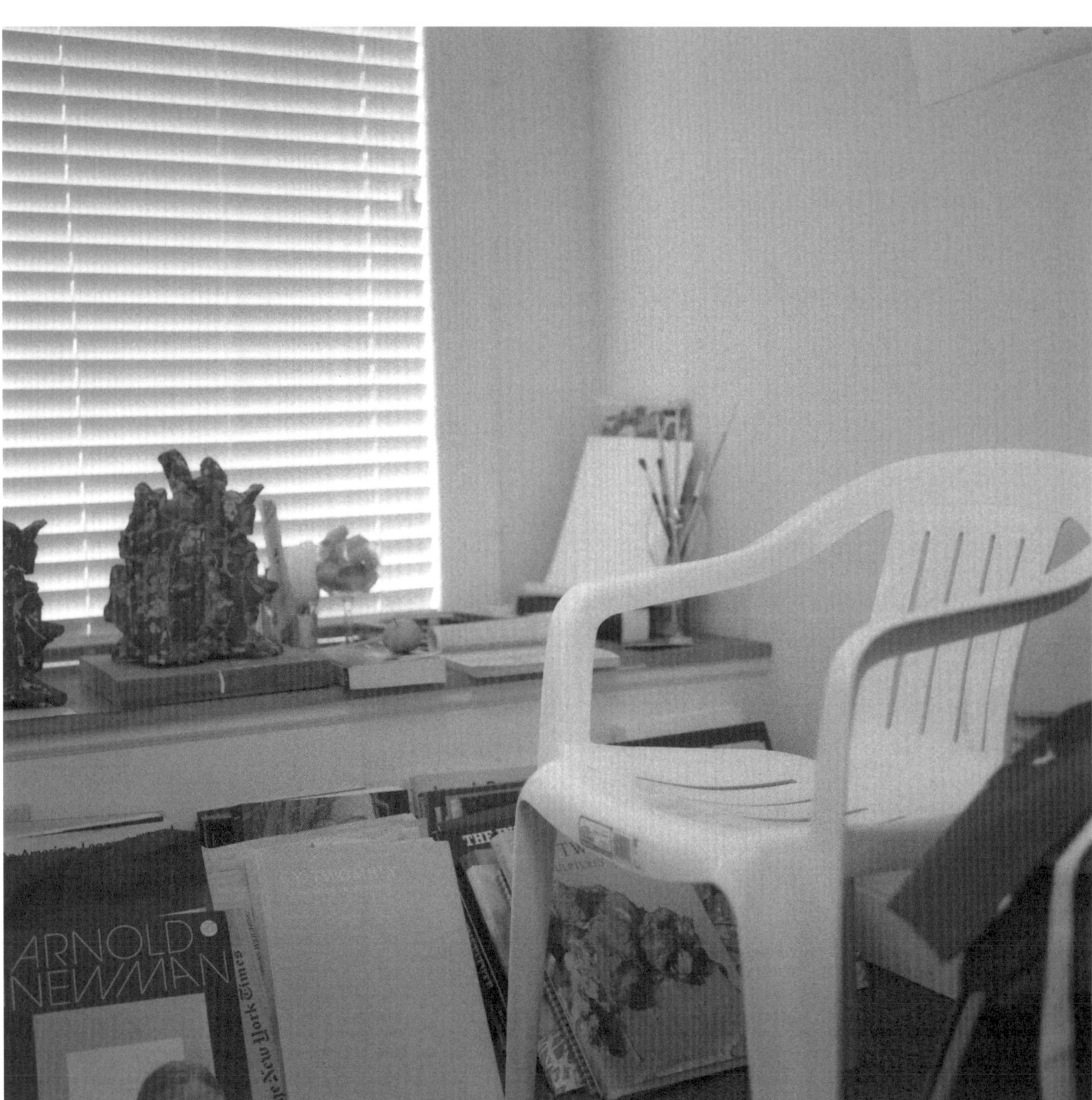
ARNOLD
NEWMAN
The New York Times

have an entirely new value as shimmering dabs of color and light. In Sally Mann's *Untitled (Slippers and Flare)* from 2005, the artist's empty shoes lie in front of the bare studio wall. Traces of Twombly's painting activity have left behind the negative outline of a picture, which suggests a white passageway into another world (of art or of death?).

Cy Twombly transformed his photographic motif past the tipping-point after which it remains recognizable only in its tiniest elements; Sally Mann transcends it to create a lucid aura. Rob McDonald does everything possible to lower the motif's charge, to "downplay" it, to understate it. With its low viewpoint, the image continues the line of Twombly's view from his Monobloc seat in the studio (he was present during the shoot). The artist's shoes lie unpretentiously in front of a workdesk on which two sculptures are blurrily suggested. Their provisional positioning suggests that Twombly might at any moment slip in and continue working on the paintings whose canvases hang in the background. In compositional terms, the shoes are picked out from the surrounding space by their position on a darker carpet. Nonetheless, this principal motif seems like a repoussoir that is intended only to lead the viewer's eye onward to the true subject of the picture. Everything that is shown alongside it (tubs of paint, postcards, boxes) is no less entitled to a presence in the pictorial space.

A similarly nonhierarchical, "decontaminating" approach also characterizes the other *Studio Still Lifes*: they too appear to lack a center, to be oddly unfocused, as if framed by chance, photographic "misses." The elements of the picture — Cy Twombly's personal objects (glasses, Polaroid camera, painting utensils), fragments of paintings, rolls of canvas, all kinds of odds and ends, packages, a roll of kitchen paper alongside plastic bowls of stirred paint, material for sculptures, an empty picture frame, Twombly's own Polaroid images of his paintings, flowers on a newspaper, the shakily scribbled inscription on a fragment of sculpture, the corner of a sculpture base — seem disconcertingly random in their piles and rows, and are unevenly lit, overlapping, fragmented by extreme close-up.

"Later, when I showed him the prints, he was drawn to the details, curious about what the camera had picked up," Rob McDonald has said. It is always the seemingly inconspicuous detail that McDonald shows us. The line of view runs almost level with the workbenches and passes to the side of objects, dwelling on what is apparently inconsequential. We are, as Talbot wrote, "arrested where ordinary people see nothing remarkable." Cy Twombly enjoyed taking trips with Rob McDonald into the countryside around Lexington. McDonald reports of this: "He appeared soothed and moved by the landscape. Conversation was beside the point, but then, 'Look at that,' he would say, gesturing to nothing in particular that I could see."

In Rob McDonald's photographs we move as if through a landscape. They reveal unexpected glimpses, pile up objects into lines of gentle hills or steep slopes, and make the canvases of painting, with their white curling streaks, appear like waterfalls. Twombly's studio space is revealed as a passage through a changing series of vistas that present the recurring objects from ever new perspectives. McDonald avoids overviews that would record the studio in a documentary way, although the entire space can be reconstructed if the individual views are placed alongside each other as a sequence. As in a natural space, one wanders through what is seen, makes unexpected connections between the objects, pauses at a chance element, discovers the inconspicuous. McDonald's photos "suggest resonance," they show "how places inhabited might be imagined to shape vision and voice." In Rob

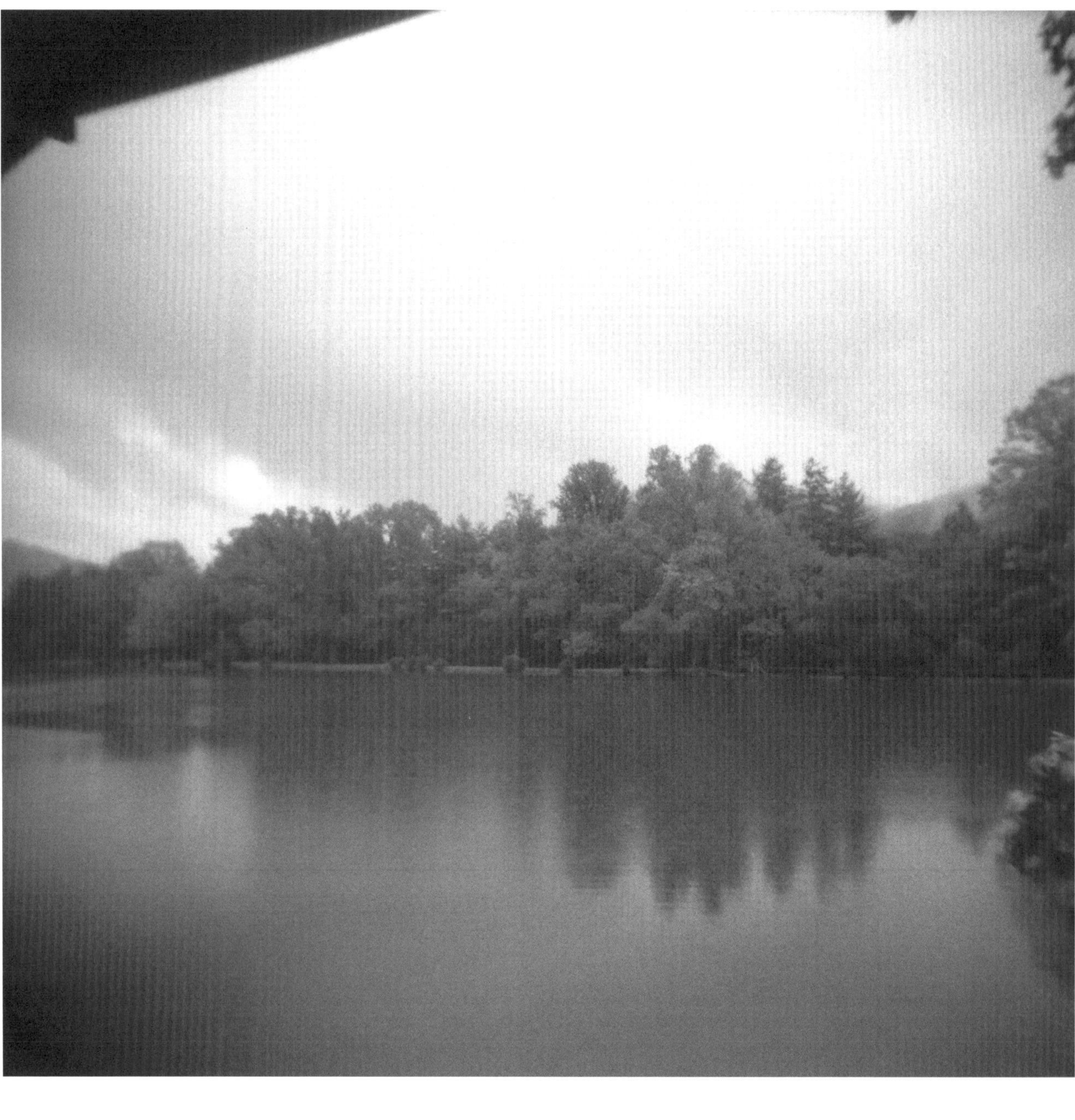

McDonald's eye, Cy Twombly's studio landscape is a place in which the artistic imagination takes form, a place that reveals itself only when it is experienced emotionally.

If considered in the categories of aesthetics, the artistic effect of the works of Sally Mann can be assigned to the category of the Sublime, which seeks an intensification of the motif, a transfiguration of what is seen. The works of Rob McDonald, in contrast, reveal qualities that since the 1770s have been described using the concept of the Picturesque. This third aesthetic category, after the Beautiful and the Sublime, is an unclassical category that was developed in relation to the English landscaped garden, and it gives heightened significance to the unnoticed detail and to values such as irregularity, chance, or roughness. While the Sublime gives an impression of "too much," the Picturesque suggests one of "too little." The landscape becomes a stimulus for the artistic fantasy, a canvas onto which the power of imagination is projected. Objects are treated as landscapes and the landscape in turn is perceived as a painting. McDonald's picturesque sensibility is manifested emphatically in the *Black Mountain College* series: the notable blurring of edges and the dark tones of the pictures evoke an optical instrument of picturesque aesthetics, the so-called Claude glass. This small, slightly convex mirror with a darkened surface made it possible to view a real landscape in the manner of a landscape painting by Claude Lorrain. What was seen appeared within a far smaller field of vision, with a picturesquely highlighted middle ground and blurred edges.

Rob McDonald understatedly calls these works, which were made in the context of his friendship with Cy Twombly, "visual documents, recordings of a very specific (and rare) place and time." But they are more than that. Not only by perceiving what is seen in a pictorial mode, but also by the picturesque sensibility of his eye for the uncharged, unfocused, the fragmented, uncomposed, the peripheral, McDonald's affinity in spirit to the principles of Twombly's art is revealed. In the intimate tact of its intentional "artlessness," giving significance to the random, the intentionally clumsy, undefined, vague, in the alternation between the transience of the gaze and the dwelling on apparently trivial details, Rob McDonald's pictorial aesthetic of resonance comes into contact — like a friend's embrace — with the art of Cy Twombly.

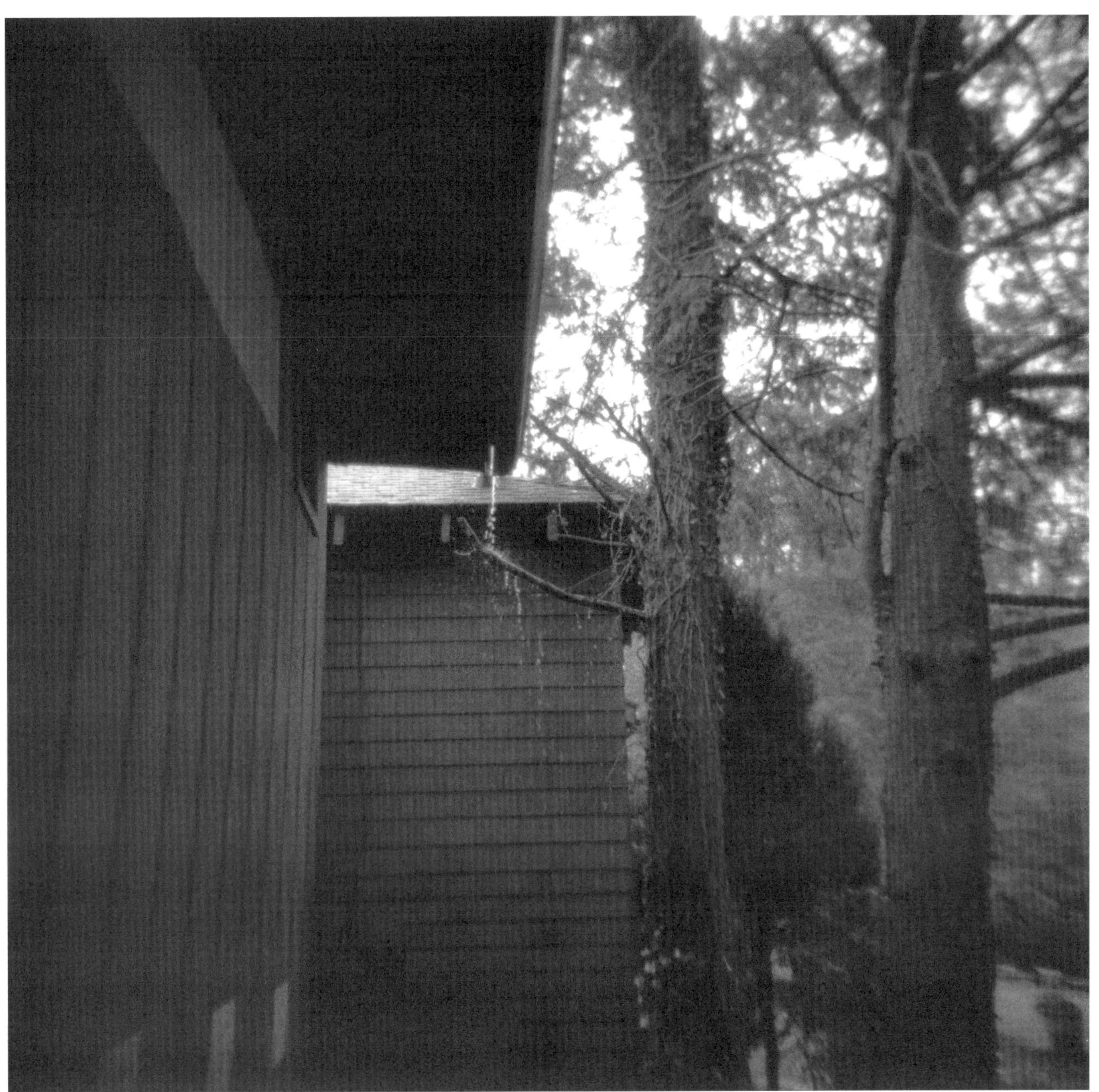

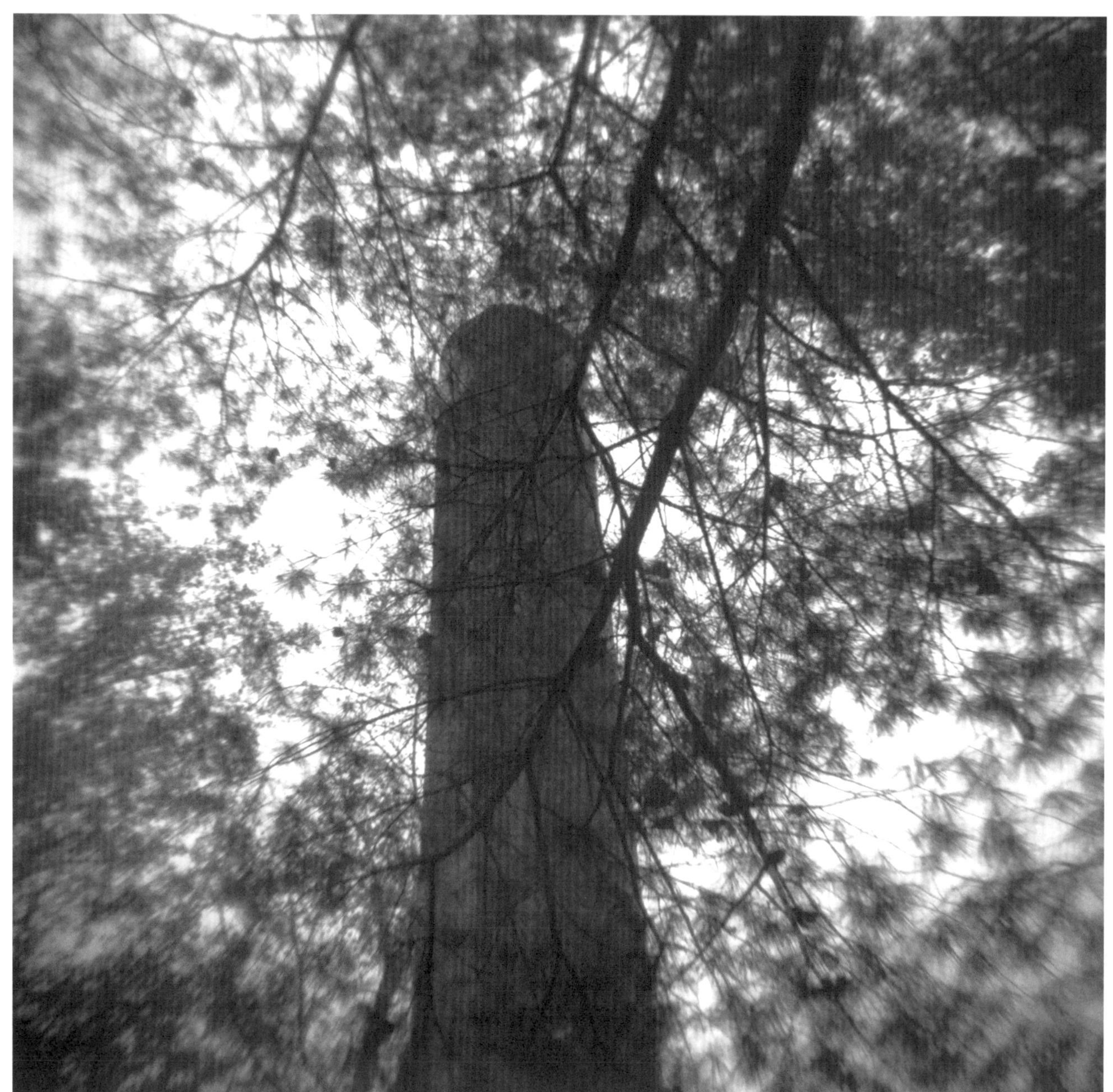

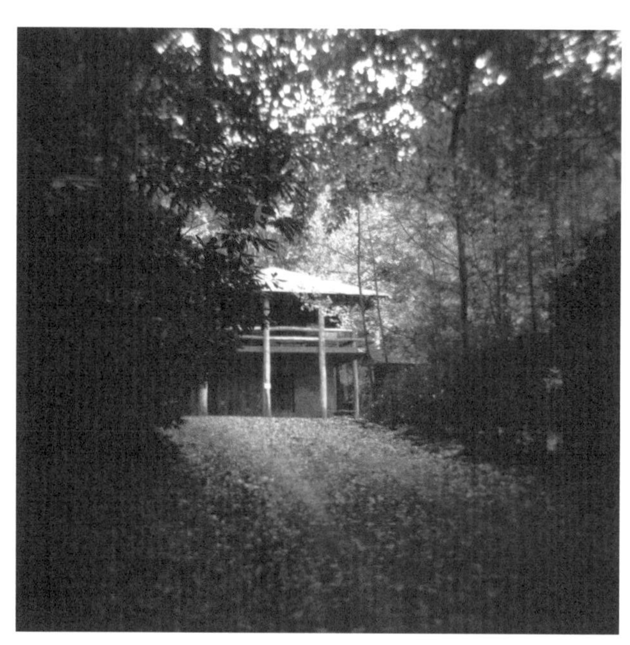

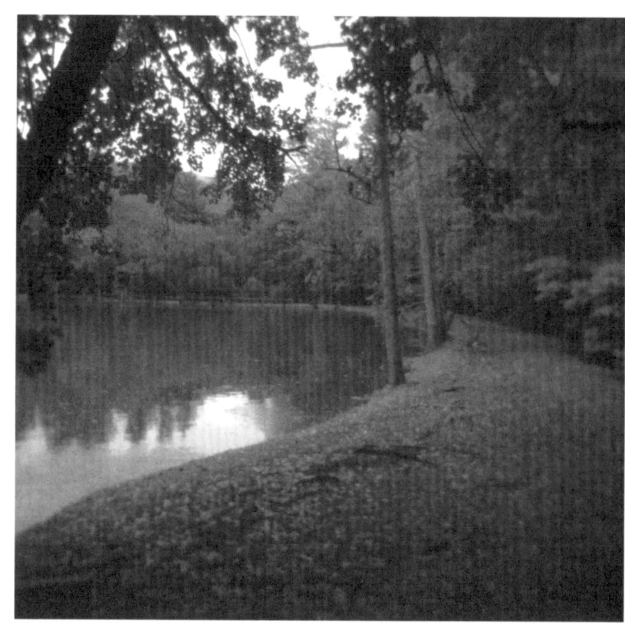

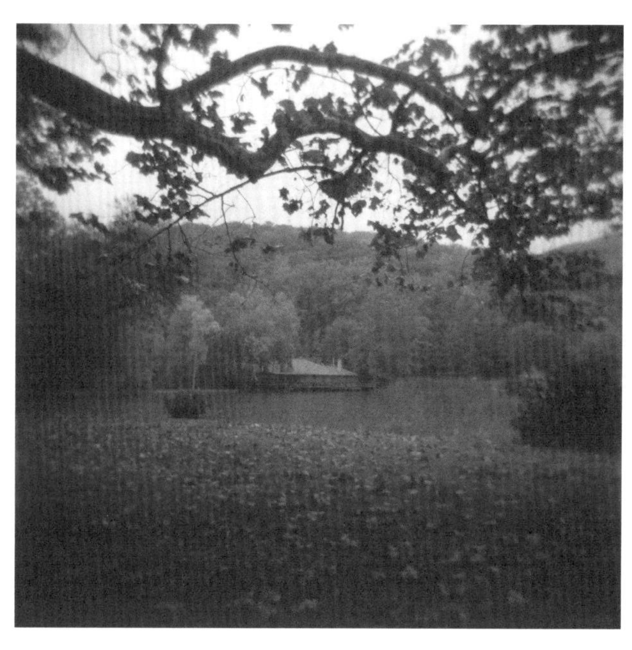

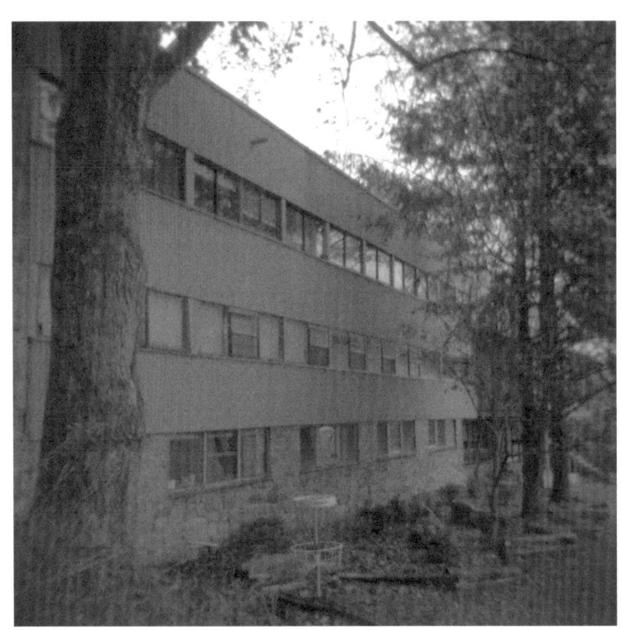

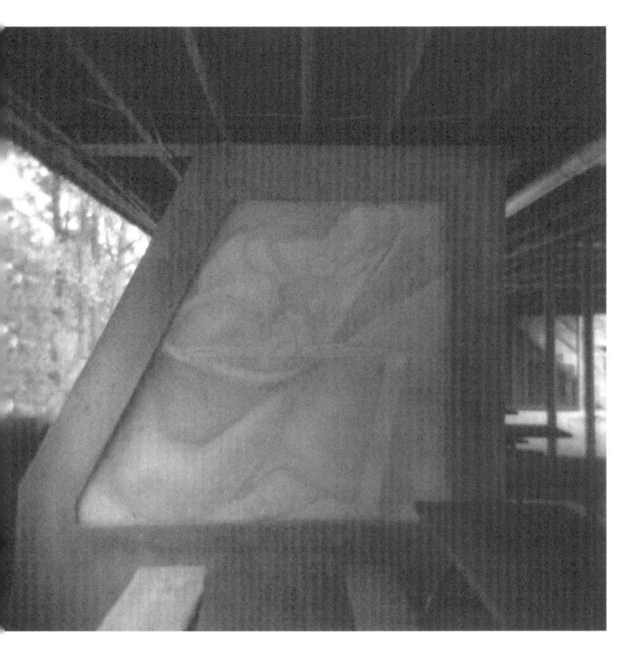

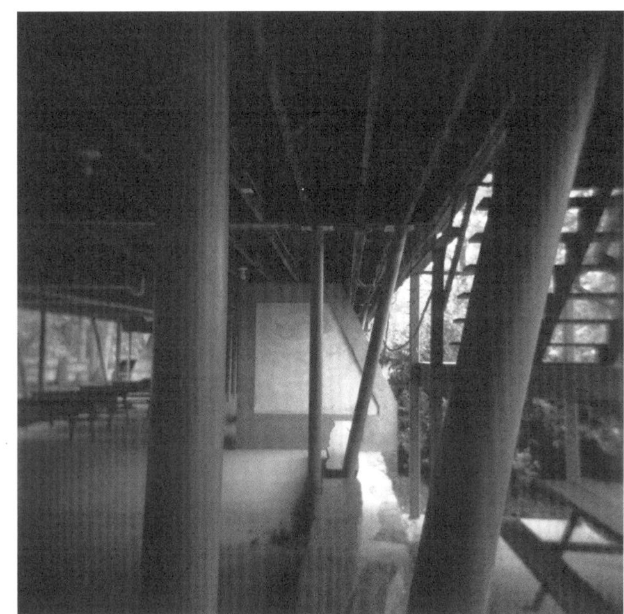

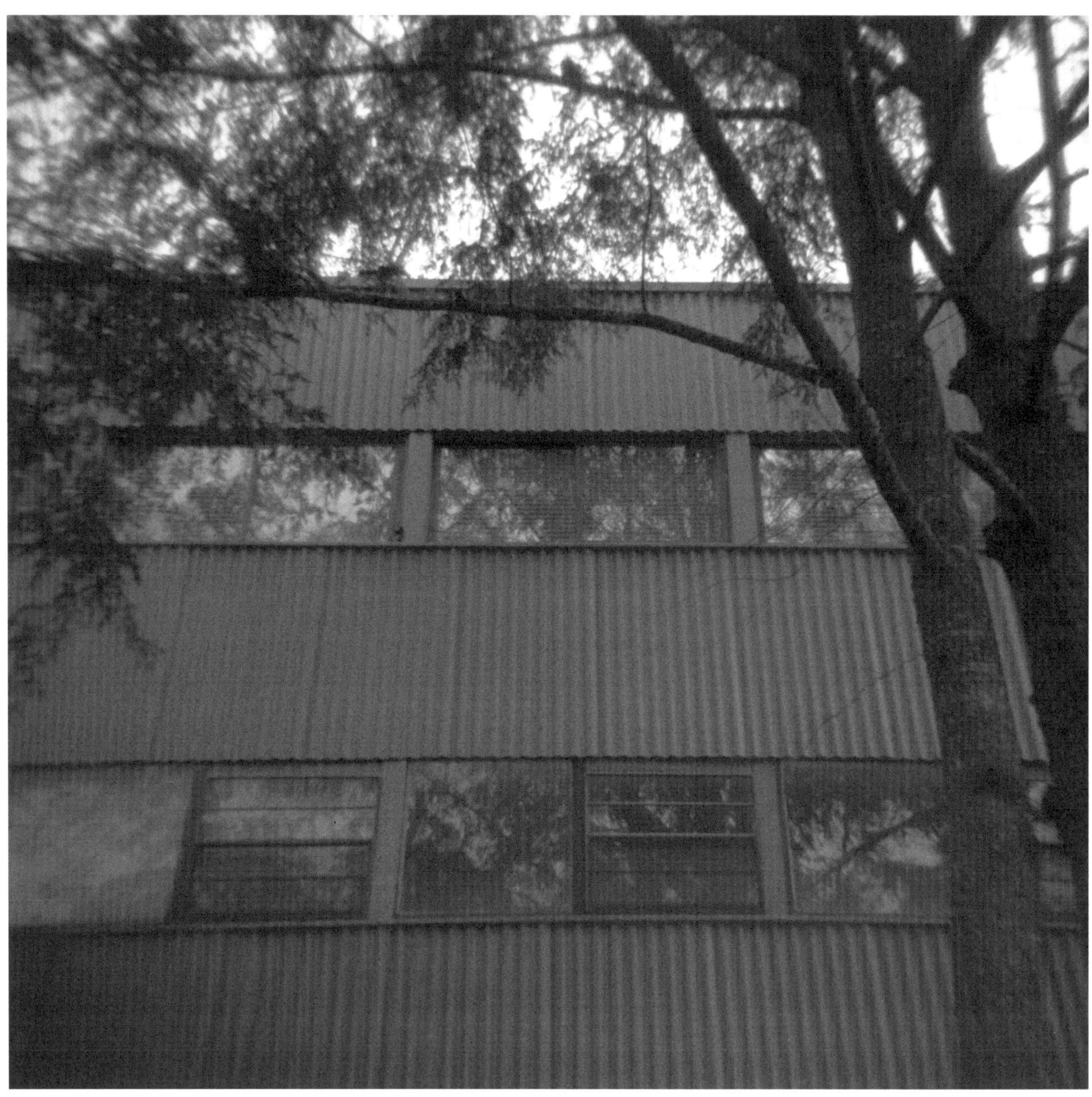

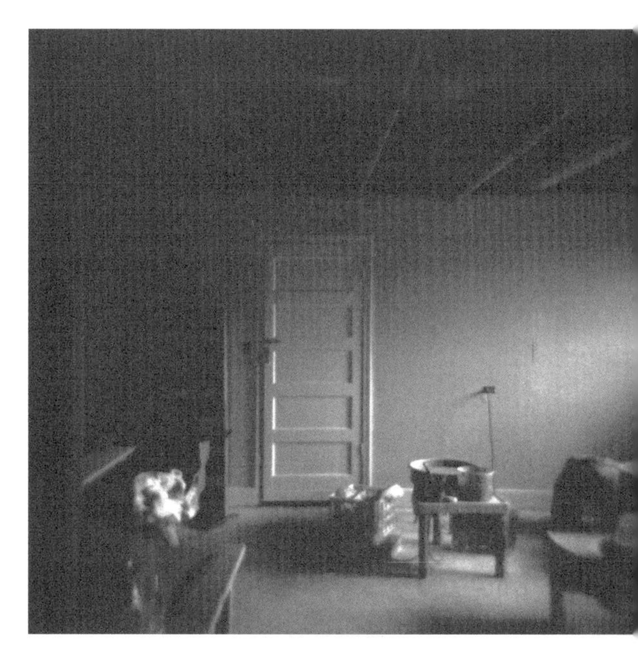

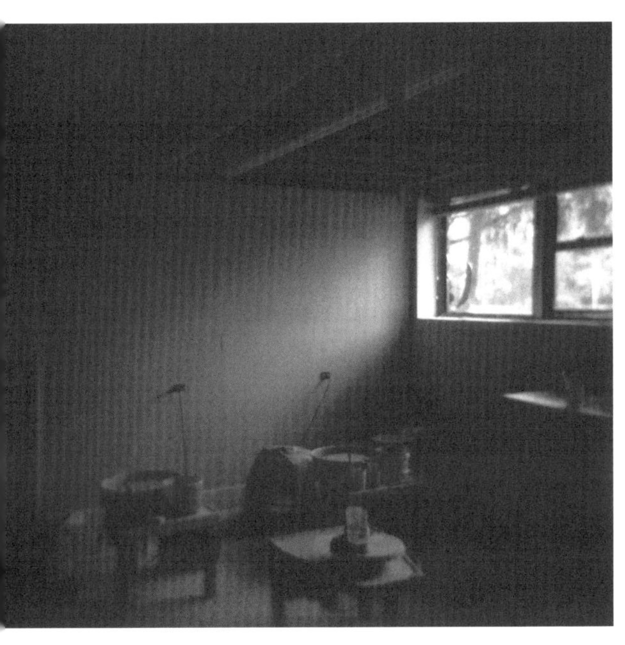

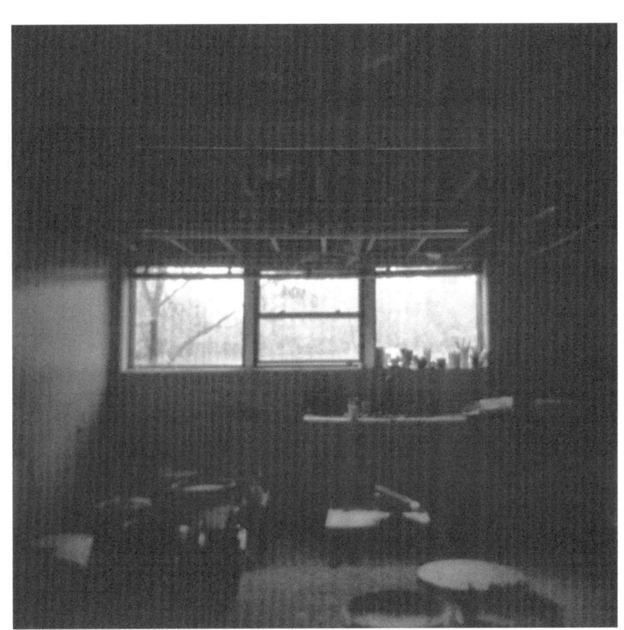

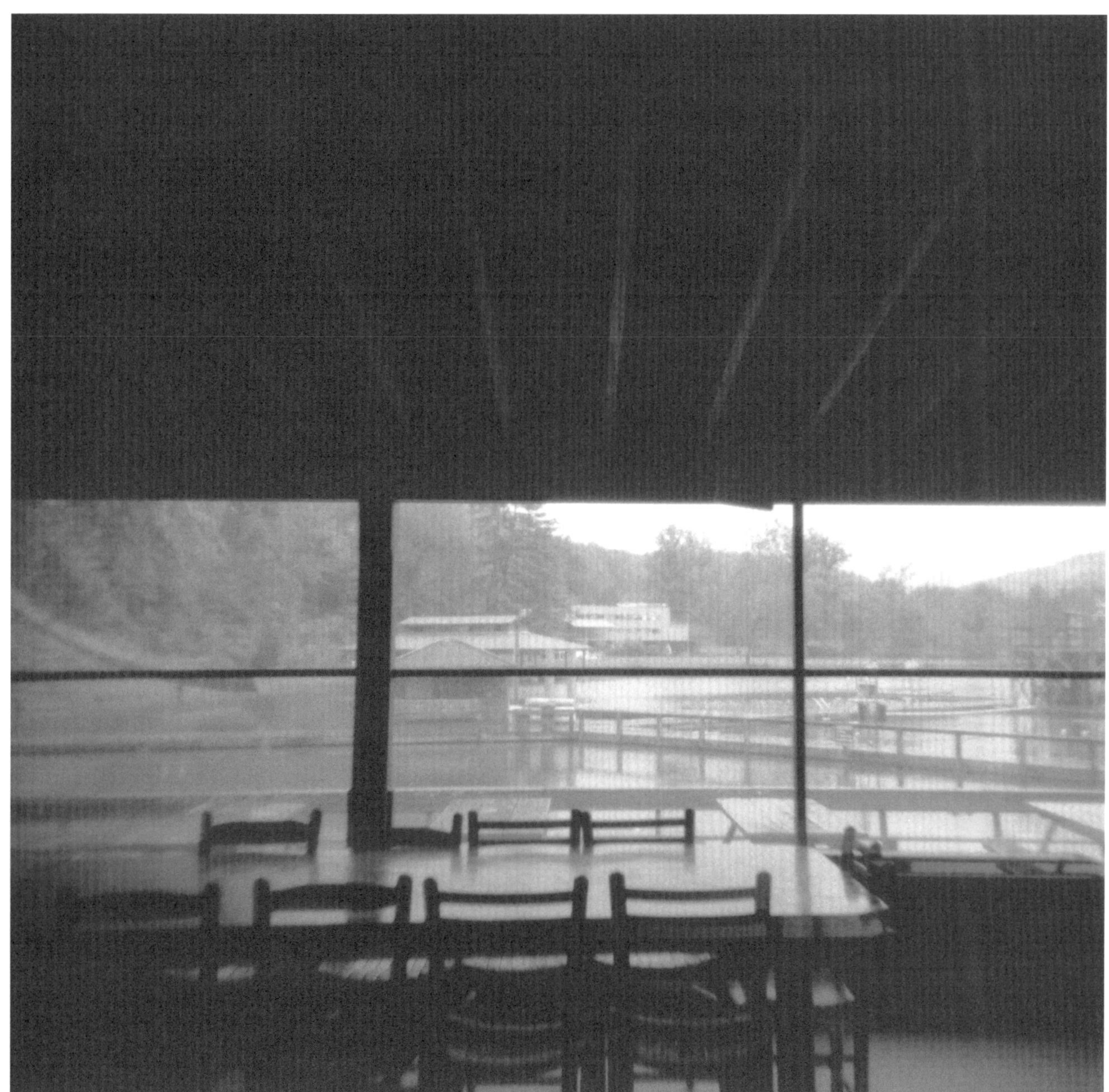

EDITORIAL NOTES

This publication presents two portfolios from the series *Studio Notes* (2007–2020).

Studio Still Lifes (2007–2008) are pigment prints on Red River Aurora Natural Cotton Fiber paper with the size of 15,24 × 15,24 (33 × 24) cm in an edition of 5 + II AP each.

Black Mountain College (2009) are pigment prints on Red River Aurora Natural Cotton Fiber paper with the size of 12,7 × 12,7 (26 × 21,5) cm in an edition of 5 + II AP each.

For detailed information on each print and other works in the series, please visit the website of the AnzenbergerGallery: anzenbergergallery.com.

ACKNOWLEDGMENTS

For many years of steadfast support, production o the beautiful premiere exhibition of *Studio Notes*, an her partnership in conceiving this book I must firs thank my gallerist Regina Anzenberger.

Through our communications about Cy Twombly Thierry Greub and Krystyna Greub-Frącz have be come not only dear friends but also valued collabora tors. They introduced me to Andreas Langensiepen whose extraordinary understanding and sensitivity are reflected in the design of this publication.

A 2013 residency at the Virginia Center for th Creative Arts allowed time and space for my firs attempts to organize and consider possibilities as sociated with the photographs I made of Cy's studi and home. A fellowship from the Virginia Museum of Fine Arts in 2019–2020 provided significant re sources to continue that work.

During his visits to Lexington, and in all our interac tions, I have appreciated the graciousness and gen erosity of Nicola Del Roscio. From the start, Sally Mann has been a sympathetic ear for musings or "my time with Cy." Over the years, a precious few friends have talked me through hesitations and res ervations and, ultimately, encouraged me to shar these photographs. I thank them for their indul gence and, most of all, understanding: Jean Brown Harry Pemberton, Bob Williams, Louis Blair, Claudi Smigrod, Erik Mace. My most important counsello in this, and all things, has been my wife, Christin Russell McDonald.

— *Rob McDonald*

NOTES TO “DRAWN TO THE DETAILS”

The quotations from Rob McDonald are taken from email conversations with the artist in spring 2023. — As well as the photographs of Sally Mann and Rob McDonald of Cy Twombly’s last studio in Lexington and Tacita Dean’s film, the documentary photographs taken in 2004/2005 by Udo Brandhorst should be mentioned, cf.: *Cy Twombly in der Alten Pinakothek, Skulpturen* 1992–2005 (exhibition catalog, Alte Pinakothek Munich 2006), ed. Alte Pinakothek, Munich 2006, 130, 133–134, 136–137. — On the Picturesque in photography see: Wolfgang Kemp: *Bilder des Verfalls: Die Fotografie in der Tradition des Pittoresken.* In: *Foto-Essays zur Geschichte und Theorie der Fotografie,* expanded edition, Munich 2006 (1978), 99–139; on the Picturesque in art, see the exhibition catalog *Pittoresk. Neue Perspektiven auf das Landschaftsbild/ Beyond the Picturesque,* ed. Marta Herford in cooperation with Steven Jacobs and Frank Maes, Herford 2009.

I thank Regina Anzenberger for requesting that I contribute a text; Rob McDonald for the wonderful collaboration; Krystyna Greub-Frącz (as always) for the inspiration; Orla Mulholland for the sensitive translation; Andreas Langensiepen for the creative book design; Walther König for his personal commitment and the inclusion of the book into the publishing program; Sally Mann for our shared conversation; Nicola Del Roscio for the friendly support. — Klaus-Peter Busse brought the exhibition in the AnzenbergerGallery to my attention; this essay is dedicated to him in friendship.

— *Thierry Greub*

BIOGRAPHIES

Rob McDonald is a Professor of English and Fine Arts and Associate Dean of the Faculty at Virginia Military Institute, Lexington.

Sam Stephenson is a 2019–2020 Guggenheim Fellow in General Nonfiction. His books have been published by W. W. Norton, Alfred A. Knopf, and Farrar, Straus and Giroux.

Thierry Greub is a Professor of Art History at the University of Cologne. His publications include three books on Cy Twombly: *Cy Twombly. Image, Text, Paratext* (Fink: Paderborn 2017); *Das ungezähmte Bild. Texte zu Cy Twombly* (Fink: Paderborn 2017); *Cy Twombly. Inscriptions, Vol. I–VI* (Brill/Fink: Paderborn 2022).

Selections from the series and the exhibition
STUDIO NOTES: *My Time with Cy*
AnzenbergerGallery, Vienna, Austria
11 May – 18 August 2023

First edition of 300 copies.
A collector's edition of 25 includes a cyanotype, "113 West Nelson Street, Lexington, Virginia (2012)," handmade by Rob McDonald, signed and numbered.

Cover: *Untitled* [CTS 4–9], 2007–2008

Book design and typesetting:
Andreas Langensiepen | textkommasatz
Concept and editing:
Thierry Greub, Krystyna Greub-Frącz
Translation from German (Essay by Th. Greub):
Orla Mulholland, Berlin

Printed with the generous support of the Fondazione Nicola Del Roscio, Rome.

FONDAZIONE
NICOLA
DEL ROSCIO

www.anzenbergergallery.com
www.robmcdonaldphotography.com

First published in 2024 by
Verlag der Buchhandlung Walther und Franz König
Ehrenstraße 4, D-50672 Köln

Printed and bound in Germany:
Lösch GmbH & Co. KG

Bibliographic information published by the Deutsche Nationalbibliothek.
The Deutsche Nationalbibliothek lists this publication in the Deutsche Nationalbibliografie; detailed bibliographic data are available in the Internet at http://dnb.d-nb.de.

Distribution:

Europe
Buchhandlung Walther König
Ehrenstraße 4
D - 50672 Köln
Tel: +49 (0) 221 / 20 59 6 53
verlag@buchhandlung-walther-koenig.de

UK & Ireland
ART DATA
12 Bell Industrial Estate
50 Cunnington Street
London W4 5HB
United Kingdom
T +44 (0)208 747 10 61
F +44 (0)208 742 23 19
orders@artdata.co.uk

Outside Europe
D. A. P. / Distributed Art Publishers, Inc.
75 Broad Street, Suite 630
USA - New York, NY 10004
Tel: +1 (0) 212 627 1999
orders@dapinc.com

ISBN 978-3-7533-0711-4